BIRTH LIKE YOU
Believe

Praise for

Birth Like You Believe

"As Christians, we are called to be in the world but not of the world (John 17:14-15). This speaks to all areas of our lives; and, in my opinion, especially in the birth space. I believe this book, *Birth Like You Believe*, is a resource to help women of faith prepare both practically and spiritually for birth. Kirstie is passionate and encouraging as a doula and childbirth educator, a wonderful guide in pregnancy and birth!"

– Imani Fitch
Labor Doula
Evidence Based Birth Instructor
and former Labor & Delivery Nurse

"I am honored to endorse *Birth Like You Believe: How to Reduce Pain in Childbirth from the Inside Out* by my esteemed colleague and phenomenal birth doula, Kirstie Foley. Her profound expertise in educating and assisting mothers during pregnancy, labor and birth shines through in this inspiring and empowering book. With her unparalleled skill and deep compassion, Kirstie guides women on a life-changing journey from fear to faith, empowering them to grab hold of the truth of God's Word in order to experience childbirth in the most transformative way. She gracefully unveils how engaging one's faith can lead to a beautiful, supernatural birthing experience. For any woman seeking to embrace childbirth with confidence, Birth Like You Believe is an invaluable resource. It will undoubtedly empower you, uplift you and encourage you to approach childbirth with a new, sacred lens that will surely lead you to experience the profound beauty and strength of bringing new life into the world."

– Jet'aime McKinney
CEO, Full Bloom Birthing Co.
Birth Doula; Doula Trainer; Childbirth Educator

"Be prepared to be informed to the highest degree! *Birth Like You Believe* is a much-needed resource that will educate, equip and empower women to truly birth supernaturally! Whether it is your first baby, or you are a repeat birther, this book will encourage you to explore the many benefits that can be achieved from implementing the principles laid out in *Birth Like You Believe*. Kirstie Foley has gracefully delivered this inspiring gift to the birthing community, with each chapter promised to be filled with insightful, actionable self-administering tools that will guide the reader whilst journeying through what often can be a difficult and tumultuous time of conception, pregnancy, labor and delivery. In addition to this fact, the author has incorporated godly principles to stir up the faith of the believing women. This book is the truest form of self-care seen in recent times, for every woman thinking about pregnancy or who is currently pregnant. It is a must-have, must-read essential that will positively impact the life of every woman that has it. "

– Tracey Goddard-Johnson
Believer in Jesus, Mother of 5 Children,
UK Registered Midwife (RM), Student Certified
Professional Midwife (CPM), Childbirth Educator
(ICCE), Certified Lactation Counselor (CLC), Certified
Resilient Model Trainer (CRM, Trauma Resource Institute)

"My Precious Spelman Daughter Kirstie, I am immensely proud of you for writing this extremely important book. I praise and glorify God for gifting you with the skills to become a certified doula. Your powerful spiritual gifts of ushering souls into God's Kingdom match your passionate gifts of assisting mothers with ushering God's precious babies into this world. God gave you a vision for this book, and I am profoundly impacted by how brilliantly it is written. It provides practical keys to unlock an understanding of childbirth from a biblical perspective. Women, and mothers-to-be; men, and fathers-to-be will benefit from reading this extremely compelling book because it serves as a spiritual guide to the birthing process. It provides profound insight regarding the importance of being filled with faith, not fear; and praying effective prayers! This book will teach readers how to manage the potential complications of pregnancy and childbirth. Additionally, women who experience the trauma of infertility and the anguish of having miscarriages will be encouraged by the words and testimonies in this book.

Thank you, Kirstie … I pray God's abundant blessings upon you and your family, in Jesus' Name.

I Love You,"

– Dr. Juanchella Grooms Francis, PhD
Senior Lecturer: Spelman College Psychology Department
Founder & Executive Director: Life Coach for Christ Ministries

"Ladies, it is a pleasure to write this endorsement for such a timely read, *Birth Like You Believe*. The title alone almost spells it out for you. Kirstie Foley is not only a woman who walks the WORD out in her daily life as a pastor and leader, she also puts the WORD to work in her entrepreneurial status as a doula. Being a doula is a very important job: it requires you to have a positive mindset, non-judgmental spirit, kind heart, an attentive ear, a firm yet soft and unwavering voice, and a strong FAITH. The act or job of being a doula can be found in the WORD of GOD, but not the word itself. However, the action of the women in the Bible who are attending the births and that's besides the midwife, are performing the task of a doula. They are there to speak life-giving words into the ear gate of mothers and their atmosphere. That is what Pastor Kirstie (as she is fondly called) is sharing in her book, how to take the LIVING WORD and utilize it in the support rendered to expectant mothers, how the WORD emboldens expectant mothers to overcome various obstacles. It's imperative that an understanding of what one believes about birth and the WORD be ascertained to marry/merge the two for a birth experience that is so desired.

Having the confidence to know that when you speak to the mountain with the FAITH that has been given you and the Power of the HOLY SPIRIT, well, that mountain has no choice but to MOVE! I trust that women will be enlightened, encouraged, and empowered by what they read which will enable them to BIRTH LIKE YOU BELIEVE. "

–Lynette Allen-Pye, CNM, CEO
Certified Nurse Midwife (CNM)
Genesis Birth Concepts Inc., CEO

BIRTH LIKE YOU
Believe

HOW TO REDUCE PAIN IN CHILDBIRTH FROM THE INSIDE OUT

Kirstie Bronner Foley

Although the author has made every effort to ensure that the information in this book was correct at the time of first publication, the author does not assume and hereby disclaims any liability to any party for any loss, damage, or disruption caused by errors or omissions, whether such errors or omissions result from negligence, accident, or any other cause. This book is not intended as a substitute for the medical advice of physicians.

ISBN: 979-8-9922646-0-9 – Paperback
eISBN: 979-8-9922646-1-6 – eBook

Library of Congress Control Number: 2024927321

∞This paper meets the requirements of ANSI/NISO Z39.48-1992 (Permanence of Paper)

1 2 2 7 2 4

Contents

Introduction   *vii*

1   Believers' Eyes for Birth   1
2   Supernatural Childbirth, Part 1:
        God in Birth   7
3   Supernatural Childbirth, Part 2:
        Freedom Defined   17
4   How Your Emotions Affect Labor   27
5   How to Evict Fear   35
6   Easy Labor?   41
7   Coping with Complications–*Like a Believer!*   47
8   Infertility   59
9   Miscarriage   71
10   How to Pray Prayers God Hears   83
11   The Birth Space   93

12   How to Birth Like You Believe, Part 1   101
13   How to Birth Like You Believe, Part 2   109
14   Formula for Success   119
15   Are You a Believer?   127

Appendix A: My Birth Stories: Hospital & Home Birth   129
Appendix B: My Family's Birth Stories   141
Appendix C: My Clients' Birth Stories, Part 1   147
Appendix D: My Clients' Birth Stories, Part 2   155
Appendix E: Prayers for Childbirth   163
Appendix F: Scriptures to Birth Like You Believe   169
Appendix G: Confessions for Birth   175
Appendix H: Definitions   179
Acknowledgments   183

Introduction

While I do believe that childbirth is just as "natural" as urinating or digesting your food, there's a powerful difference in childbirth: new life is born. This means that God, the giver of all life, cares about the way you give birth. As a daughter of God, you can usher glory and miracles in your childbirth as you learn to birth like you believe.

Hi! I am Kirstie Foley. I'm a Christ-follower, wife, mom of two, certified labor doula and childbirth educator, founder of Powerful Peace Doula Care, and an ordained minister. Nicknamed "The Praying Doula," I specialize in comfort for the body, soul, and spirit, combining both physical techniques and spiritual support for pregnancy, labor, and the early postpartum period.

You will find *Birth Like You Believe* to be a short, easy read, written with pregnant mamas in mind! Because pregnancy hormones breed brain fog and fatigue, long books can be intimidating: but, I've got you, Sis! I've been there, haha. This one is palatable right where you are!

I encourage you to read this book while you're simply preparing for the future, trying to conceive, or already pregnant. It's important to prepare your mind in advance and to rehearse some things you will learn in *Birth Like You Believe.*

When a mama goes into labor, it's not just her body going into labor, but it's her entire being. We are spirit beings who possess a soul and occupy a body. The soul is composed of the intellect, emotions, and will. I believe in preparing your whole being for childbirth–body, soul, and spirit.

Since our internal state directly impacts our external sensations, *Birth Like You Believe* digs into the spiritual and emotional layers of childbirth, strengthening the ROOT for some sweet FRUIT in labor.

I believe that faith without works is dead and that we should do our best and trust God to do the rest! This means, even for childbirth, we need not approach it as a bodily function alone. It is a divinely created means of birthing LIFE into the world! And life never comes at a low price.

Look at Jesus' sacrifice on the cross for our divine opportunity to be "born again" spiritually and to have the opportunity of eternal life. (Now, thank God we don't have to literally die in order to bring forth new life because Christ already did that for us! In fact, it doesn't even have to be a sorrowful experience for us … but we'll dig into that later. Childbirth inevitably requires sacrifice, but there is great beauty to be found in this type of sacrifice.)

Nevertheless, we should not approach childbirth only as a spiritual experience. We do have bodies that we should nurture in [1]preparation for childbirth as well. Preparation for your mind and body are very important in addition to preparing your spirit.

As women of God, we do not have to experience childbirth like one who does not know God. We have something different inside that has power to affect our bodies and souls–the Holy Spirit. With Creator God invited to the party, so to speak, our childbirth experiences should look different.

His fingerprints should be on it–evidence that God is an active member of your birth team. Don't just say you believe in God and then birth a baby with your faith in the back seat and fear in the driver's seat. Keep reading, Daughter of God, and learn how to birth like you believe.

Disclaimers:

1. Not all women are called to biological motherhood. Some are called to be adoptive mothers, foster mothers, or spiritual mothers.
2. The concepts you will learn in *Birth Like You Believe* are applicable to all kinds of birth, whether physiological (vaginal, unmedicated) birth, medicated vaginal delivery, instrument-assisted delivery, or planned/unplanned cesarean section delivery.
3. My birth philosophy is as follows:
   a. I believe that God's original design for birth is best: unmedicated, vaginal delivery left undisturbed by man-made interventions. However, when medical interventions are

---

[1] See *Powerful Peace Birth Course* at www.powerfulpeacedoula.com

needed for health and safety, they are blessings for which we should be grateful. In
short, things in life don't always go as we
expect; and we cannot control everything
in life, not even in childbirth. In *Birth Like
You Believe,* you will learn how to invite the
hand of God on your birth for the desired
outcome as well as for any obstacles along
the way.

1

Believers' Eyes for Birth

The name "Eve" literally means "life." This tells us that women were originally created as life-givers! We are the ones gifted to conceive life, carry life within our wombs, and deliver life from our very bodies. Through our bodies, miracles happen, precious little humans grow, and purpose is multiplied.

Sometimes the world paints the picture of children and childbirth like inconvenience, pain, and suffering. Negativity surrounding childbirth can seem so magnified that women begin to wonder if it's worth the constant sacrifices for the rest of their lives!

So let's take a moment to reframe children and childbirth from a believer's perspective.

The Bible says that children are a blessing and a heritage of the Lord, a gift and reward (Psalm 127:3). Children are some of the greatest gifts on Earth because they are *life*. Creator God is the only one responsible for giving such good gifts as children, since the Bible says that every good and perfect gift comes from God (James 1:17), the giver of all life.

By the media and others' traumatic experiences, childbirth has been framed to be something fearful, dreadful, and excruciatingly painful. On the contrary, it is a privileged process uniquely crafted by God. Not every woman will give birth, but for those who do, it is an honor that grants us a glimpse of God as Creator God.

We get the opportunity to witness God creating life within our wombs, to feel the baby moving inside of us, and to watch our bodies gracefully expand to accommodate a second life within. What a special wonder, designed by God Himself!

We are the clay; He is the Potter (Isaiah 64:8). He molds our bodies into whatever our babies need, even creating a temporary organ to nourish our babies–the placenta. Wow, what a design!

The same way many industrialized nations have perverted food, this world has perverted childbirth. Many people can no longer differentiate between genetically modified food and natural food the way God created. The modifications to our food save time and generate more money but also lead to increased sterility, among other harmful effects. Unfortunately, what has been normalized is not always what is natural or healthy.

As for childbirth, women have widely been persuaded to view medicalized birth as normal, underestimating the power she has to birth babies using her body alone. Before the existence of medical interventions, hospitals, and trained doctors, women were giving birth and mankind was multiplying.

With unnecessary uses of medical interventions and greedy systems, childbirth involves more long-lasting side effects, longer recovery periods, and increased trauma. (Disclaimer: When *necessary*, medical interventions are blessings! But, they are not always necessary.)

The more medical interventions that are used, the more money childbirth makes for those who reap the benefits. Drugs and surgeries make more money for the medical system than natural childbirth! And sometimes what makes the institution more money is *not* what's best for the mother and her baby.

Other flaws of the medical system are due to ignorance of the natural birth process because medicalized birth has become "the norm." Various practices hinder the functionality of women's biological labor process. For example, within medicalized birth, mothers are often encouraged to remain in bed. With medication, IV fluids, plus electronic fetal monitoring, mobility becomes restricted to the cords connecting mom to various gadgets, not to mention drugs that make mobility risky. Movement is essential to the [2]physiological labor process! When mom moves her legs and pelvis, the baby has more space to move and to more easily navigate the birth canal.

Other issues arise due to impatience of how long the physiological birth process can take. The faster moms deliver their babies, the sooner another patient can fill that hospital room, increasing the amount of money that the hospital

---

[2] Physiological (adjective): unmedicated, vaginal childbirth without man-made interference

makes. Additionally, some medical professionals use the drug Pitocin/Syntocinon to accelerate labor contractions, attempting to shorten labor without legitimate medical need to do so. Or, the hospital system can be hasty in recommending a c-section delivery. The medical system often labels a mom's labor "failure to progress" when the reality is "failure to WAIT." Thus, medical interventions artificially accelerate labor, which can introduce complications.

More broadly, sin has tainted childbirth. We see this starting in the curse of mankind in Genesis chapter three after Adam and Eve committed the first sins. (See the chapter, "Supernatural Childbirth, Part 2: Freedom Defined" to read more about the curse of sorrow in childbirth.) Because of sin, we notice damaging effects of impatience, greed, racism, and [3]fear-mongering in the medical system surrounding childbirth.

But, childbirth belongs to God. It is His creation. Because Father God owns childbirth, why not invite His Holy Spirit to flood your childbirth experience?

Think about it like this: The Word says that our bodies are not our own because we were bought with a price (1 Corinthians 6:19-20). Our bodies are the temples of the Holy Spirit, and God created our bodies. These same bodies are often abused by humans, perverted, and polluted physically and spiritually. As we have the option to devote our bodies to

As we have the option to devote our bodies to God, we also have the option to devote our childbirth experiences back to God.

---

[3] Fear-mongering (noun): manipulation that exaggerates risks to evoke fear in the victim to persuade him/her towards a targeted decision

God (in purity, sanctification, and health), we also have the option to devote our childbirth experiences back to God.

As it relates to perspective shifts, remember that your state of mind in labor directly affects your emotions, hormones, and labor progress itself. This is why it's vital to view birth in a positive light. Who doesn't want a *shorter* labor and delivery with less tension and pain?!

If your perspective of birth is negative, your emotions will reflect that and you will experience less of the hormone oxytocin that aids labor contractions and improves your mood. In response to the emotions you choose to entertain, your brain will secrete hormones that will either help or hinder labor progress.

Please remember, your brain does not control you: you control your brain! You have the power to train your mind for birth. Because of the brain's neuroplasticity, it can rewire itself based on learning and experience. That means, what you learn in this book and in [4]childbirth education can physically change your brain with enough repetition!

> *In response to the emotions you choose to entertain, your brain will secrete hormones that will either help or hinder labor progress.*

Dr. Caroline Leaf, a Christian neuroscientist, wrote the book [5]*Switch on Your Brain: The Key to Peak Happiness, Thinking, and Health* that includes her 21-day brain detox

---

[4] See *Powerful Peace Birth Course*: www.powerfulpeacedoula.com
[5] See my Amazon store (www.powerfulpeacedoula.com/products) to purchase your copy of *Switch on Your Brain: The Key to Peak Happiness, Thinking, and Health* by Dr. Caroline Leaf.

> *Replace toxic, fearful thoughts with God's heart for childbirth and the beautiful possibilities that lie within.*

plan. Although this book covers rewiring of the brain in general, many women need to learn how to rewire their brains towards childbirth specifically! Replace toxic, fearful thoughts with God's heart for childbirth and the beautiful possibilities that lie within.

And you will find that some of the same principles you will embrace to enhance your birth experience will also elevate your overall health–mentally, physically, and emotionally. It's not just part of you in labor, but all of you. And what you once thought was mostly a physical act is actually very emotional and spiritual, going much deeper than our mere bodies.

Sister, let's reclaim childbirth from the world's version of it. Claim YOUR birth for the Kingdom of Light, reminding yourself WHO designed childbirth and how blessed you are to be a bearer of life. Open your eyes to understand how your pregnancy, labor, delivery and postpartum season can and should look different from that of the mothers of the world. With the King of Glory in the equation, add love, subtract fear; add peace, subtract anxiety; and multiply God's power with your preparation for a heavenly welcome for your precious newborn!

2

Supernatural Childbirth, Part 1: God in Birth

*C*hildbirth cannot be separated from God because He is the giver of life. In childbirth, God grants women the privilege of also being givers of life, after His likeness.

When new life is born, the Kingdom of God notices. He is omnipresent, everywhere at the same time, meaning God is there in every childbirth. The question is, by the way you choose to birth, will you notice Him?

> *When new life is born, the Kingdom of God notices.*

Christian women view childbirth very differently from one another, and some view it exactly the same as unbelievers. Whether you currently see it as a natural process of life, a condition that warrants medical attention, a spiritual experience, a terrifying milestone, or an exciting adventure, remember God.

Where is God's place in your childbirth experience? Have you limited His presence based on a lack of knowledge or a lack of faith? Does your perspective of childbirth include only natural elements? Have you considered supernatural elements in your birth experience?

Is your personal definition of supernatural childbirth limiting to God? Some believe that supernatural childbirth can only exist in the absence of pain and/or medical interventions. Others view supernatural childbirth as a birth experience in which God intervenes, with or without the presence of pain or medical interventions.

I believe that childbirth is both a spiritual and a natural experience. "Supernatural" encompasses both the spiritual (super) and the physical (natural) elements of birth. God–Creator of the Heavens and the Earth, the universe and all that is in it–designed childbirth personally. He made womens' bodies to birth babies just as "naturally" as our bodies are made to digest food or have a bowel movement.

What makes some believers' births feel supernatural while others feel only natural? FAITH. Based on the faith of the mother, she might encounter more supernatural elements that elevate her birth experience. Often, God will meet you at your level of faith. Some moms have better experiences on their second or third childbirth because they dared to BELIEVE God for more.

I believe that a supernatural childbirth experience happens when you put the "super"–God's power–on the "natural"–our bodies, minds, and strategies. I believe it is a combination of both faith and works–doing your best to prepare and trusting God to do the rest!

[6]Prepare your body, soul, and spirit for childbirth according to His original design before we had modern medicine; yet prepare your heart to trust God no matter what. Put your faith in God, not in your body, your plan, or your doctor/midwife. Anything outside of God Himself can fail, but God never does.

Ideally, a supernatural childbirth experience would look like this:

1. Perfectly healthy pregnancy
2. Spontaneous onset of labor
3. Unmedicated vaginal delivery without the use of medical interventions
4. Peace, strength, and power of the Holy Spirit empowering mom
5. Perfect health for both mom and baby

Sometimes, supernatural childbirth does look like the above scenario. God could physically accelerate labor progress with rapid [7]dilation (opening) of the cervix, a quick descent of the baby in the pelvis, or even help the baby to rotate into optimal positioning for delivery in unusually short timeframes. For some, supernatural childbirth is even experiencing labor and delivery without pain during contractions!

However, I choose not to limit my personal definition of supernatural childbirth to this perfect set of circumstances. Why? Because humans and man-made systems are flawed, but God is limitless.

Let's discuss these three factors in birth:

---

[6] See *Powerful Peace Birth Course*: www.powerfulpeacedoula.com

[7] Dilation (noun): the opening or widening of the cervix during labor to make enough space for babies to exit the uterus

1. Human error
2. Maternal healthcare systems
3. Omnipotent God

Women's bodies are not as they were in the beginning of Creation. Now, there is man-made pollution plus perversions of natural food. Even the modern working lifestyles inhibit

Humans and man-made systems are flawed, but God is limitless.

optimal body positioning as women sit at desks all day or recline on couches. Mom can influence her baby's position by her own posture while seated, standing, and exercising! (See [8]*Powerful Peace Birth Course* to learn more detail about how to encourage optimal fetal positioning.)

Exercise, chiropractic care, and proper maternal positioning (during the day as well as while sleeping!) directly affect the positioning of babies in-utero which impacts the intensity and duration of labor, as well as the probability of successful vaginal delivery. For example, when babies are head-down facing mom's spine, labor is often shorter and less painful than other fetal positions in the uterus. And breech babies (feet/bottom-down) lead to c-section delivery or slower, more painful labor in many cases.

In the beginning of Creation, women's lifestyles increased their chances of having a well-positioned baby because they were active. Their posture was often better than the posture of people who look down at cell phones

---

[8] See *Powerful Peace Birth Course* at www.powerfulpeacedoula.com to learn more about optimal baby positioning, among many other birth topics.

and laptops and sit down in vehicles through hours of traffic. They did not have modern conveniences and had to work manually to wash clothes, gather food, and travel by foot! Walking is excellent preparation for labor, and women in the early days of humankind walked daily.

Another factor in modern times that degrades our childbirth experiences is what we ingest. In the early days of humankind, everything was organic and non-gmo! Genetically modified organisms did not exist, and science was not impacting the quality of our food at all.

With genetic modifications to food–removing their ability to reproduce–and women eating crops that have been polluted by pesticides and degraded by depleted soil (in countries like the U.S.), what does it mean to believe the saying "You are what you eat"?

Next, let's briefly discuss the impact of the maternal healthcare system wherever you live. Some systems better facilitate [9]physiological (unmedicated, vaginal) birth than others. For example, in some countries, medical providers are more commonly trained in breech delivery (when a baby's bottom, feet, or both bottom and feet are delivered first).

However, in the U.S., breech delivery is commonly a lost art, along with instrument-assisted delivery (forceps/vacuum). Broader training expands mothers' options for vaginal delivery in complicated scenarios.

Limited training often leaves cesarean section delivery (AKA c-section) as the primary resort when the baby is malpositioned or mom is experiencing a dangerously long pushing stage. And this is also why one-third of births in

---

[9] Physiological (adjective): unmedicated, vaginal childbirth without medical interventions

the U.S. are cesarean sections, with one-third of those deliveries being medically unnecessary c-sections.

While we hope to prepare our bodies for labor without complications, we cannot always avoid them. Some maternal healthcare systems are better equipped to handle complications while still facilitating vaginal delivery. Others resort to c-section delivery too quickly with many common variations of normal birth. There is more than one definition of a normal birth!

In some maternal healthcare systems, undisturbed labor and delivery is scarcely observed. Part of the system is to intervene throughout the process, which is rooted in their fundamental birth philosophy–viewing childbirth as a medical procedure rather than as a normal bodily function.

Pregnancy is not a disease, disorder, or an illness to be treated. When left undisturbed by man-made devices and returning to God's way of birthing, childbirth can be exactly what it was designed to be (whenever possible). Birth locations that lend better to undisturbed childbirth tend to be birth centers and homes (in many industrialized nations).

However, not all moms are great candidates for out-of-hospital births due to high-risk factors or financial barriers as it relates to insurance coverage. Ultimately, undisturbed childbirth is the goal: but, when medical interventions are needed for the health and safety of mom and/or baby, the hospital system is best for that family.

Let's face it: not all childbirth experiences will be the same; not all mothers' bodies are the same; not all babies are the same; and not even any two pregnancies in one mom's life are guaranteed to be the same!

Omnipotent God does not need perfection from women,

doctors, nurses, midwives, doulas, babies, or even a perfect healthcare system in order for Him to highlight beauty in or from any childbirth experience.

God is sovereign, and He has no limits, despite flawed humanity and man-made systems. I believe that supernatural childbirth is one in which the glory of God ("super") is reflected in women's bodies and babies ("natural") during childbirth. His glory in our bodies results in labor progress.

This labor progress could be physical, emotional, mental, spiritual, or a combination of them all! It could be experienced in an abundance of peace even if the circumstances don't seem to warrant peace. It could be joy, where mom finds herself laughing in labor, even in the midst of intense labor contractions!

> *I believe that supernatural childbirth is one in which the glory of God ("super") is reflected in women's bodies and babies ("natural") during childbirth.*

As I previously stated, God could physically accelerate labor progress with rapid dilation (opening) of the cervix, a quick descent of the baby in the pelvis, or even help the baby to rotate into optimal positioning for delivery in unusually short timeframes. For some, supernatural childbirth is even experiencing labor and delivery without pain during contractions!

Supernatural childbirth does not always mean that birth goes according to mom's plan; but it does mean that Almighty God intervenes with His sovereign plan!

Examples of supernatural childbirth possibilities:
Not limited to the scenarios listed

1. No pain during contractions
2. No pregnancy, labor, or [10]postpartum complications
3. Healing of pregnancy complications, leading to safe delivery
4. No adverse side effects from pain medications (e.g. epidural/opioids, etc.)
5. Turning of malpositioned baby during labor, in time for a vaginal delivery
6. No adverse side effects from [11]cesarean section delivery, including easy recovery
7. Abundant [12]peace in mom's soul in the presence of concerning circumstances

God can do anything. His power knows no boundaries. One of my life's mottos is "Do your best and trust God to do the rest," and I encourage you to believe like this for childbirth. As my father says, "Work like it's all up to you, and pray like it's all up to God."

Again, I encourage you to [13]prepare your body, soul, and spirit for childbirth according to His original design before we had modern medicine; yet prepare your heart to trust God no matter what. Put your faith in God, not in your body, your plan, or your doctor/midwife. Anything outside of God Himself can fail, but God never does.

---

[10] Postpartum (adjective or adverb): the period following childbirth
[11] See Appendix B, "My Family's Birth Stories," for my mother's supernatural c-section birth experience.
[12] See Appendix D, "My Clients' Birth Stories, Part 2," for a testimony of this example scenario.
[13] See *Powerful Peace Birth Course*: www.powerfulpeacedoula.com

When you think about your birth story, take a look at history. His story–the Bible–tells us that God is always faithful and that all things work together for good to those who love God and are called according to His purpose (See Romans 8:28).

Birth plans fail, but God never fails. No matter what detours your birth may take, know that all things will

> *Birth plans fail, but God never fails.*

work together for your good, Daughter of God. And it might be that your birth story turns out BETTER than you expected that it would, or that it actually does match the plan you outlined! It could be that, after birth, you discover that God used your experience to birth a new you that's better suited for your destiny.

The bottom line is this: invite God into your pregnancy and birth experience and make His presence known. Then TRUST Him. He is worthy of your trust, and He is able to deliver! ASK Him what you want; and trust that, if your request is in His will, you will have it.

1 John 5:14-15 (NKJV)

"Now this is the confidence that we have in Him, that if we ask anything according to His will, He hears us. And if we know that He hears us, whatever we ask, we know that we have the petitions that we have asked of Him."

God has ALL power in His hands, and He can defy the odds. The essence of who He is defies the odds! Unless God gives you a glimpse of your birth story in advance, you will find out during the adventure. So, buckle up, strapping yourself in the car, so to speak, using the belt of truth (God's Word) as your seatbelt (Ephesians 6:14), the gospel of peace on your feet (Ephesians 6:15), your preparation as the wheels, your faith as the gas, and then let Jesus take the wheel and DRIVE.

3

Supernatural Childbirth, Part 2: Freedom Defined

God does not desire for us to suffer in childbirth. It is not punishment for womankind … anymore, that is. Pain and suffering are two different things. God designed the uterus as a powerful muscle that contracts during labor to perform the following functions (summarized):

1. Open your [14]cervix
2. Rotate your baby
3. Push baby through the birth canal

---

[14] Cervix (noun): the opening of the uterus, located on the bottom of the uterus. This is where babies exit the uterus during labor.

> *A labor contraction is pressure with a powerful purpose!*

Like an intense workout at the gym, flexing the muscle of your uterus does not have to equal sorrow. In fitness, we talk about a so-called "good burn" in our muscles; and while childbirth is usually far more intense than the average workout, it is pressure with a powerful purpose.

Although the terminology "supernatural childbirth" is not found in Scripture, the concept is based on Scripture. To me, supernatural childbirth is all about breaking the curse of sorrow in childbirth as written in Genesis chapter three.

So let's take a look at Scripture: In Genesis 3:16 (KJV) the Word says, "Unto the woman he said, I will greatly multiply thy sorrow and thy conception; in sorrow thou shalt bring forth children …"

As you can see, sorrow in childbirth was part of the **curse** upon womankind after Adam and Eve introduced sin into the world. Then Jesus became a curse *for* us, by dying a criminal's death on a cross–although He was sinless, perfect and innocent.

Galatians 3:13-14 (ESV)
"Christ redeemed us from the curse of the law by becoming a curse for us—for it is written, 'Cursed is everyone who is hanged on a tree' —so that in Christ Jesus the blessing of Abraham might come to the Gentiles, so that we might receive the promised Spirit through faith."

Because of Jesus' sacrifice on the cross (made from a tree!), His followers do not have to live under curses, even longstanding generational curses. But we, through faith in

Christ, have the power to break those curses and exercise our faith to live a more abundant life.

But please understand: As believers, we do not automatically experience the benefits of God's Word and His promises without exercising our faith. Years ago, my sister Neiel (Bronner) Zimbron repeated something that stuck with me: "Faith activates the promises of God in your life."

As it relates to childbirth, this means that daughters of God do not have to birth under the curse. We can use our faith to claim redemption from any curse! Some Bible translations use the word "pain" in place of "sorrow" in the curse on childbirth; however, the original Hebrew uses two different words for this idea in Genesis 3:16. It reads: "... I will greatly multiply thy _____ and conception; in _____ thou shalt bring forth children ..."

The first blank represents the Hebrew word "itsabon." It is most closely translated as "sorrowful toil," the same word used in Genesis 3:17 as God cursed the ground for Adam's sin. Again, here, the word "itsabon" is more closely translated as "sorrowful toil," which makes much sense in the context of anguish in the hard work of providing food for one's family or in the woman's context–sorrowful toil of hard work in childbirth. If it specifically meant physical pain, it would not so easily relate to the same pain the man experiences in the curse of the ground.

Genesis 3:17 (KJV)
"And unto Adam he said, Because thou hast hearkened unto the voice of thy wife, and hast eaten of the tree, of which I commanded thee, saying, Thou shalt not eat of it: cursed is the ground for thy sake; in sorrow shalt thou eat of it all the days of thy life."

The second blank in the paragraph above represents

the Hebrew word "etseb," which is also translated to mean either "pain" or "sorrow," but many sources verify that it most closely means "sorrow" or "grief," indicating emotional pain more than physical pain of labor.

Thankfully, Jesus has already carried our sorrows by His act of redemption on the cross, freeing us from bondage to sorrow or grief.

Isaiah 53:4-5 (ESV)
"Surely he has borne our griefs and carried our sorrows; yet we esteemed him stricken, smitten by God, and afflicted. But he was pierced for our transgressions; he was crushed for our iniquities; upon him was the chastisement that brought us peace, and with his wounds we are healed."

We can infer that the curse refers more specifically to emotional pain for both the woman in childbirth and the man while working to provide for his family, all due to the consequences of sin.

Also in the curse of Genesis 3:16, we see the word often translated as "conception": "... I will greatly multiply thy sorrow in conception ..." This word in Hebrew is "herayon" and is translated both as "conception" and "pregnancy." This explains the anguish, toil, and sorrow that often accompanies the process of conception and pregnancy when women continue to live under the curse! By faith, we now can command all health challenges and sorrows of conception *and* pregnancy to submit to the power of God.

Whether you believe that the curse referred to physical pain, emotional grief, or both, we know that because of Jesus' sacrifice on the cross, we are not bound to pain or sorrow in childbirth. And whether or not our bodies experience pain in labor, our souls are free to experience the peace and joy of God that does not submit to conditions of the body.

Regardless of what's happening in your body, your inner self does not have to be bound by outward circumstances. You can be renewed on the inside during labor!

I often say, "In childbirth, a baby is not the only thing that's born: a new mother is also born." When a woman births God's way, she may experience a rebirth of herself, a new version of self

> In childbirth, a baby is not the only thing that's born: a new mother is also born.

that has emerged from this transformational milestone. She may be more mature, faith-filled, resilient, and confident! In contrast, when the enemy has his way in childbirth, a traumatized, wounded mother is born.

Several years ago, my sister Neiel introduced me to the idea of supernatural childbirth after experiencing a [15]supernatural childbirth herself: a pain-free labor and delivery filled with the peace of God. She later recommended to me a book called *Supernatural Childbirth* written by Jackie Mize, which I highly recommend to all Christian women who desire to have children. This book laid a powerful foundation for my faith surrounding childbirth.

Before I had my first child, I thought supernatural childbirth referred exclusively to "pain-free" childbirth (in addition to fear-free). I prayed and believed that I, too, would have a pain-free childbirth experience. By the time

---

[15] See Appendix B, "My Family's Birth Stories," to read Neiel's testimony of supernatural childbirth.

I experienced pain in labor—while fully resting in faith—I began to think that perhaps I was not getting that supernatural childbirth that I requested from God.

Those thoughts didn't get too far before I realized that God absolutely showed up in many ways during my labor, delivery, and recovery. Because of the undeniable supernatural elements in [16]my childbirth experience, I realized that I did have a supernatural childbirth!

Yes, I experienced pain, but I experienced no sorrow. In the midst of the pain, I had peace that surpasses all understanding (See Philippians 4:7) and unspeakable joy (See 1 Peter 1:8). I experienced no fear, even as a first-time mom. Even the nurses and the [17]obstetrician marveled at my confidence and composure, which I know came from a Source beyond myself. My soul felt anchored in God, and no matter how long I labored, my soul was never shaken.

I had prayed for perfect peace, perfect love, fearlessness, joy, and an unmedicated vaginal birth: My God absolutely answered.

Because of my experience, I decided that the definition of supernatural childbirth that I once believed was far too limiting for my limitless God. How could humans tell God that experiencing pain disqualifies an experience from being supernatural? Don't Spirit-filled Christians experience God's supernatural power throughout our lives, although our lives are not void of pain?

God did not answer my prayer for pain-free labor with a "yes" either time I gave birth. But He did answer "yes" to all of my prayers for my soul and spirit during labor,

---

[16] See Appendix A, "My Birth Stories."
[17] Obstetrician (noun): a surgeon who specializes in medical interventions for childbirth and is trained to manage both high-risk and low-risk pregnancies from a medical perspective

not to mention my prayers for unmedicated vaginal births without the use of pain medication, medical induction, or forceps/vacuum. Additionally, my [18]perineum did not tear either time! Praise God!

I never experienced pain that was more than I could bear. I never felt tempted to request pain-relief medication, even through the most intense moments. It was not for the motivation to prove a point that I avoided pain medication: I didn't request it because I knew I could persevere without it. I did not feel like I was having a near-death experience. God empowered me to manage the intense pressure of the contractions both spiritually and physically through comfort techniques. And truly, I had already made up my mind before labor that I was going to give birth without medication and its associated risks.

I never felt hopeless when my first labor dragged on for nearly forty hours. God was clearly with me. (And thankfully, my second labor was much shorter!)

In my second labor experience, I remember a moment in active labor when I started laughing with unspeakable joy and excitement that I was finally about to meet my baby boy! I went from laughing to crying tears of joy as I labored in my basement. I had a planned home birth, and I had intentionally saturated my basement in prayers, creating a holy sanctuary for God to inhabit in preparation for my childbirth experience.

Because I was in the midst of intense contractions, no one could convince me that I felt that way because I was so strong in myself–just God! After I met my son, the

---

[18] Perineum (noun): the tissue connecting a woman's vagina and anus

[19]midwife kept telling me to talk to my baby because I was still in my labor zone, simply repeating "Thank You, Jesus" while holding and kissing him. My heart was overflowing with gratitude. My labor zone was worship!

As you listen to or read the experiences of other believers who experienced supernatural childbirth, remember that God is sovereign and He does not make a lot of carbon copies. Do not expect your birth to be identical to that of another's. Decide what you wish to believe God for in your own childbirth experience and meditate on supportive scriptures. Build your faith, reach for the stars with your prayers, and praise God for wherever you land!

Build your faith, reach for the stars with your prayers, and praise God for wherever you land!

You might experience a completely pain-free birth! Or you might experience manageable pressure that is not more than you can bear with Christ's help. But, the reality is this: God is not a genie in a bottle. He is not obligated to answer every prayer with a "yes"; and He purposefully plans different journeys for His daughters–in life and in childbirth. However, God is consistently FAITHFUL, all-powerful, all-knowing, ever-present, and overwhelmingly GOOD.

As long as you believe in Jesus Christ and live like one of His disciples, you, too, can claim the promises of God. You can break curses in your life in numerous areas, even

---

[19] Midwife (noun): a medical professional who delivers babies of low-risk pregnancies and performs clinical tasks for childbirth, specializing in vaginal birth and natural techniques for delivery

when it comes to pregnancy and childbirth. You can experience the supernatural touch of God on your birth experience giving you the power to [20]birth like you believe!

1 John 5:14-15 (ESV).
"And this is the confidence that we have toward him, that if we ask anything according to his will he hears us. And if we know that he hears us in whatever we ask, we know that we have the requests that we have asked of him."

---

[20] See Part 1 and Part 2 of the chapter "*How to* Birth Like You Believe" to learn practical steps towards supernatural childbirth.

4

How Your Emotions Affect Labor

$\mathcal{W}$ hat if I told you that happiness could progress your labor? Or that fear could slow it down and make it more painful? Did you know that remaining peaceful during labor is not just for emotional comfort but is biologically productive for labor progress?

If you fail to mentally prepare for labor and simply "hope" to feel calm, you're too late. Now is the time to invest in your inward woman and have a foundation on which your soul can climb during labor.

Not only should you prepare your body, but also you should prepare your mind, emotions, and your spirit.

> *Your perspective of childbirth and your preparation process directly affect your emotions during labor.*

Your perspective of childbirth and your preparation process directly affect your emotions during labor.

Your mind, emotions, and your spirit all work together during labor to facilitate more efficient contractions or to yield more painful, less effective contractions. Now, let's discuss the biological factors supporting this truth.

The hormone oxytocin is the driving force of labor, stimulating uterine contractions. Your uterus is a powerful muscle that contracts in response to the hormone oxytocin, also known as the "love/bonding" hormone.

Oxytocin is produced in the hypothalamus of the brain and then released by the pituitary gland into the bloodstream. Its release is signaled by sexual activity, warmth, breastfeeding, and gentle touch. It thrives in environments of intimacy, affection, safety, dim lighting, and cuddly babies!

Adrenaline, on the other hand, is one of the "fight or flight" hormones that is released into the bloodstream during times of stress and fear. It triggers physiological responses like increased heart rate, blood pressure, and blood sugar levels.

In scenarios when we are in danger and need to run or fight immediately, adrenaline and cortisol are our friends! But in childbirth, high levels of these stress hormones delay labor progress and can even increase the risk of hemorrhage (excessive blood loss).

Let's take a look at this cycle:

1. Fear or stress leads to the release of adrenaline.
2. Adrenaline (and other stress hormones) leads to tension in the body, contradicting the release and yielding processes needed for birth.
3. Tension increases pain and the chances of your genitals tearing in the pushing stage.
4. Adrenaline counteracts oxytocin.
5. Lower levels of oxytocin result in less effective uterine contractions.
6. Less effective contractions delay or stall labor progress.
7. Delayed/stalled labor progress increases the risks of more medical interventions like synthetic oxytocin, medicinal pain relief, instrument-assisted delivery, and cesarean section delivery, each of which introduces more risks and complications.
8. Remember, stress hormones like adrenaline and cortisol increase blood pressure and heart rate while also dilating blood vessels and increasing blood flow/output.
   a. Higher blood pressure combined with dilated blood vessels and accelerated heart rate pumps blood out of the body at faster than usual rates during stages of labor like the delivery of the baby and the placenta, sometimes resulting in hemorrhage.

Now, let's return to God's way of giving birth. When you birth like you believe, you engage your faith over fear and command your soul to be covered in that "peace that surpasses all understanding" (Philippians 4:7).

> *Faith is not the antidote to fear: love is. And we use our faith to activate perfect love in our lives through Jesus.*

Faith is not the antidote to fear: love is. And we use our faith to activate perfect love in our lives through Jesus.

"There is no fear in love; but perfect love casts out fear ..." 1 John 4:18 (NKJV).

God is love. And He is Perfect Love. When we invite the Holy Spirit into our pregnancy journey and into the birth space with us, perfect love is present. We consciously acknowledge His presence through prayer, praise, worship, and scriptures.

When you birth like you believe, fear has no place. When you make your birth space a place of worship consecrated unto God, your birth environment is automatically conducive to oxytocin release. Invite God into your birth space and love on Him with your words, your attention, your choice of music, and your heart's affection. The loving environment of worship directly increases your oxytocin flow. Oh, what intimacy when you dwell in the secret place of the Most High and abide under the shadow of the Almighty (Psalm 91:1) during labor!

And oh, what safety, confidence, and strength when you remember that "... He is my refuge and my fortress: my God; in Him will I trust" (Psalm 91:2 KJV) and remember that "The Lord is my rock ..." (Psalm 18:2).

Use scriptures to renew your mind, thereby transforming the way you think and feel (See Romans 12:2). You will find great power in meditating on God's Word. Repeat related scriptures so many times during pregnancy that God's Word surfaces in your mind during labor. Also, you can post scriptures on the walls of your birth space or use [21]scripture cards to divert your attention to God's Word.

Additionally, remember the power of people! God loves to use people, so do not isolate yourself during pregnancy or labor. Don't assume that you can do this on your own or "just me and God." Allow God to use people to encourage you, affirm you, and compliment you. Invite the right people in your life and into your childbirth experience; and be honest with them when you feel weak, exhausted, or discouraged. (See "The Birth Space" chapter to learn more about the kinds of people you should invite to your birth.)

Let God use others to facilitate gentle touch and physical affection for more oxytocin! God did not create us to function best alone, just as He stated in Genesis 2:18 (NKJV) about Adam, "... It is not good that man should be alone."

As we discuss oxytocin, you must be careful not to confuse our natural (God-made!) oxytocin with synthetic oxytocin. Synthetic oxytocin is known by various brand names ([22]Pitocin or Syntocinon) and often referred to as simply "oxytocin" or "PIT" in the medical system.

However, there's an important difference as it relates to our mind and emotions in labor (among many differences!). While synthetic oxytocin can stimulate

---

[21] See www.powerfulpeacedoula.com/products for scripture cards.
[22] See Appendix H, "Definitions," to learn more about Pitocin.

uterine contractions like natural oxytocin, it cannot cross the blood-brain barrier to signal the release of endorphins in our bodies.

Endorphins are "feel good" chemicals in our brains that are natural painkillers and stress-relievers. Endorphins are released in our brains during exercise, and they help to keep us coming back to the gym for more even when it burns. Those same endorphins serve to help us through the most intense parts of labor!

Without our natural painkillers, physiological childbirth is much more difficult to achieve. Quite literally, synthetic oxytocin intensifies contractions without increasing your ability to cope with the intensity. God-made oxytocin uses increasing levels of endorphins to help women cope with increasing intensity of contractions. And women's bodies were not designed to experience increasing intensity of contractions without correspondingly rising levels of endorphins!

Women's bodies were not designed to experience increasing intensity of contractions without correspondingly rising levels of endorphins!

God's design is amazing! And as you learn more about the biological process of childbirth, you will also begin to identify more flaws in the medicalized version of childbirth. Man-made counterfeits often solve one problem while creating another issue (risks and side effects). Because human inventions are flawed, they will never be able to adequately compete with the design of Almighty God. Some risks of synthetic oxytocin include hyperstimulation (over-working) of the uterus, uterine rupture (uterus tearing), and fetal heart rate abnormalities or fetal distress.

Disclaimer: Medical interventions like synthetic oxytocin can be an answer to prayer in times when there is a legitimate medical need for it, rather than using it out of impatience or ignorance of the physiological labor process. It should always be used as a back-up plan after natural options are first explored.

When you, Daughter of God, birth like you believe, your faith and corresponding actions will engage your emotions in ways that produce oxytocin during childbirth, leading to better labor progress both physically and emotionally.

5

How to Evict Fear

"For God has not given us a spirit of fear, but of power and love and a sound mind" 2 Timothy 1:7 (NKJV).

The media has created a terrifying narrative surrounding childbirth, evoking fear, dread, and anxiety among moms-to-be. On television and in movies, we watch women scream to the top of their lungs when giving birth, while nearly injuring their partner's hand, haha!

Fear of birth leads some women to avoid motherhood altogether, while leading other women to increased pain and suffering during childbirth. Fear breeds tension and signals the release of the hormone adrenaline.

Tension reduces the effectiveness of labor contractions and increases pain. Tension can also lengthen labor. And, adrenaline counteracts oxytocin, the hormone responsible for uterine contractions and for signaling endorphins, our bodies' natural painkillers. Approaching birth with fear increases the risk of a traumatic birth experience!

Unfortunately, birth trauma has become so common that moms share horrific stories as if their experience is normal. There is a difference between the terms "common" and "normal." Traumatic birth is common, but it is not normal. However, you, Daughter of God, need not fear having a traumatic birth experience.

Trauma is not God's will for childbirth. God's will for childbirth involves joy and peace as new life is born! Trauma tends to lead moms down dark paths of depression, anxiety, shame, regret, anger, hopelessness, and fear. This is not God's will for mom–a giver of life–nor is it God's will for precious babies to be born into environments stained by trauma. Children are very spiritually sensitive!

> *Trauma is not God's will for childbirth. God's will for childbirth involves joy and peace as new life is born!*

Childbirth is often viewed as a physical experience only; but in reality, it is inseparable from a spiritual experience (whether the participants realize it or not). When a mom's soul gets wounded in childbirth, she enters a spiritual battle that threatens to steal her joy. This spiritual battle tempts her to view herself as a victim and forget that she is "more than a conqueror" through Jesus Christ (Romans 8:37) and that God has made her to be a "joyous mother of children" (Psalm 113:9).

In some situations, moms are technically victims in childbirth: victims of obstetric abuse, malpractice, or victims of medical systems tainted by greed, racism, or ignorance of the physiological birth process. Moms can even feel like victims of their own ignorance of the medical system or of the birth process. However, Daughter of God, you do not have to be victimized in your soul because you have victory in Christ Jesus.

Our enemy, the devil, thrives in trauma, wounds of the soul, and seeks to tempt mom to inhabit demonic spirits of depression, anger, fear, hopelessness, and more ... Satan loves for babies to be born into environments that are robbed of the joy of bringing forth new life. He wants moms to be so traumatized that the selfish nature of pain prevents them from being the lights in their homes that they were designed to be.

It's mighty difficult to be patient with others when you're emotionally traumatized in addition to being sleep-deprived and sore, also with achy, engorged breasts, sore nipples, a ravenous appetite, raging hormones, and a new "mom bod" you must learn to love.

Traumatic birth experiences lead moms to increased fear for the next birth; and for some, it leads them to stop reproducing. God tells us to "... Be fruitful, and multiply, and replenish the earth ..." (Genesis 1:28), and it is not His will that fear thwarts that mission.

Reproduction is in the will of God, as we see in Genesis 1:28. (Reproduction can be both physical and spiritual, so this is not to condemn those who do not have biological children.)

Daughter of God, cling to scriptures to eradicate fear and command your soul to bless the Lord (Psalm 103:1). You can do all things through Christ Who strengthens you (Philippians 4:13). You were designed by Almighty God to birth babies into the world, and He has equipped you with all that you need to do so.

You will find your power for fearless childbirth in Christ

alone. Remain connected to Jesus as your power source, plugging into Him daily through prayer, Scripture, praise, worship, and other godly women.

> *There is no mountain He cannot move or empower you to climb.*

The same God who makes joy, peace, and strength available to you throughout life is able to do the same for your childbirth experience. There is nothing impossible for God (Matthew 19:26). And there is no mountain He cannot move or empower you to climb.

Psalm 18:29 (ESV) says, "For by You I can run against a troop, and by my God I can leap over a wall." This means that there is no obstacle, no challenge you cannot overcome with God! You CAN do hard things with God on your side. In Him, you are victorious, and you win, Sis!

Let God train your spiritual muscles to climb the mountain of childbirth with power in your soul and wisdom for your mind and body. So, do your best to prepare your body and mind through [23]education, physical preparation, and labor support. And press into God for spiritual preparation.

Through Christ, you've got this, Sis! Fear, who? Leave fear and trauma for those without faith and put God back on the throne of your childbirth experience.

John 14:27 (NKJV)
"Peace I leave with you, My peace I give to you; not as the world gives do I give to you. Let not your heart be troubled, neither let it be afraid."

---

[23] See the *Powerful Peace Birth Course* at www.powerfulpeacedoula.com

I promise you that He rules with peace, grace, and power to quench any fiery darts thrown your way.

When you invite God to rule over your [24]perinatal season, you've simultaneously invited perfect love to rule. Childbirth is all about LOVE. It is quite literally a "labor of love"! When the God who is perfect love permeates the atmosphere, fear cannot survive. "There is no fear in love, but perfect love casts out fear" 1 John 4:18a (ESV).

> *When the God who is perfect love permeates the atmosphere, fear cannot survive.*

Herein, the key to eradicating fear in childbirth is fostering an environment for the soul, spirit, and body to bask in the perfect love of God. Anchor your deep breathing in the peace of His presence–the Prince of Peace! Let Him lead you beside the still waters and restore your soul (Psalm 23:2b-3a).

Form a habit of commanding your soul how to feel, as David did in Psalm 103 (KJV): "Bless the Lord, O my soul, and all that is within me, bless His holy name." Tell yourself, "Soul, bless the Lord!" And as you bless Him, praising Him, His Word tells us that He inhabits the praises of His people (Psalm 22:3).

This promises His people that, when we praise God, He will show up. And when He shows up, perfect love is in the room and so is perfect peace! In the presence of the Lord is fullness of joy (Psalm 16:11), and fear receives its eviction notice.

---

[24] Perinatal (adjective): the period of time spanning pregnancy and the postpartum season

6

Easy Labor?

*B*abies–life itself–are not cheap.

The Merriam-Webster dictionary defines the word "labor" as "expenditure of physical or mental effort especially when difficult or compulsory." Other sources define labor as simply "work" or even "hard work."

The word "supernatural" is not synonymous with the word "easy." Even pain-free childbirth experiences often involve challenges in pregnancy or in the postpartum period, in motherhood itself, or in a combination of them all!

You might be praying for pain-free childbirth. And trust me, God still does miracles on the earth, including pain-free childbirth! Or, you might ask God for a birth experience filled with His peace and exempt from any pain that's more than you can bear. Whatever the request, know that God's power can change anything! But don't forget that, since God is a good Father, not all tests, lessons, or milestones are "easy."

We all know that the most valuable things in life are worth fighting for and are available only at a high price. Even the free gift of salvation came at a high price paid in Jesus' blood, and then Christ-followers pay a high price to maintain our deliverance throughout life's temptations, distractions, and hardships.

My first childbirth experience helped me to *live* the lesson that the most valuable things in life are worth fighting for, AKA laboring for. Why would I expect to receive one of the greatest gifts of my life for free?

After almost forty hours of labor, I had the revelation that I could not expect to receive something this precious for a low price. For my first childbirth experience, I originally expected a pain-free birth. That was my prayer among many other prayers …

> *Our faith will never facilitate an outcome that is not in the will of God for our lives.*

I wanted an easy labor, void of pain and exempt from the *need* for patience. After reading about other women's stories of pain-free birth, I thought that, as long as I had the faith for it, I would experience that, too. Yes, I absolutely had the faith for it, and I believed it was going to happen for me.

However, our faith will never facilitate an outcome that is not in the will of God for our lives.

1 John 5:14-15 (NKJV) says, "Now this is the confidence that we have in Him, that if we ask anything according to His will, He hears us. And if we know that He hears us, whatever we ask, we know that we have the petitions that we have asked of Him."

Prayer will not change God's will, but it works to usher His will into manifestation. Matthew 6:10 (NKJV) says, "Your kingdom come. Your will be done on earth as it is in heaven." Scripture teaches us in the model prayer of Matthew chapter six that we can pray God's will down from Heaven to earth. You can think of prayer like a fishing rod, with faith as the bait. In this analogy, the water represents your life, and the fish represent opportunities within the will of God for your life. Only the fish in this water are able to be caught, not the fish in a different lake!

Just like everyone's life journey is different, women's childbirth experiences are different. And the Lord intends for it to be this way! God has a purpose for every child, every childbirth experience, and every mom. For a different purpose comes different circumstances, which is why God's will is not identical for every woman.

Thankfully, my second birth experience was much shorter and easier than the first, but I learned valuable lessons.

My first childbirth experience provoked me to think about the high price Jesus paid on the cross with *His* natural life, for *our* eternal life. (I sure felt like I paid a high price for my daughter and wanted to cling to her with everything within me!) And now, because of His unmatchable sacrifice, we have the opportunity for eternal life in Heaven and abundant life on this earth.

But Jesus' path was not free of pain. His life on earth was rich with wisdom, miracles, healing, deliverance, and salvation, yet also stained with pain and sorrow. Isaiah 53:3 (NKJV) describes Him as "a Man of sorrows and acquainted with grief."

Now, because the curse is broken and Jesus bore pain and sorrow *for* us, we don't have to experience that same kind of sorrow. We are not bound to pain, suffering, nor fear. We can labor for LIFE, something beautiful and amazing. And yes, it's hard work; but because of Jesus' sacrifice, it does not have to be sorrowful work.

We can have joy in the journey. We can have peace, even when it doesn't seem possible. We don't have to be humiliated, even if we poop on ourselves in labor, haha! He already suffered humil-

> *Yes, it's hard work; but because of Jesus' sacrifice, it does not have to be sorrowful work.*

iation, dread, anxiety, and torture *for* all of His children, which includes women as we give birth.

2 Corinthians 5:21 (NLT) says, "For God made Christ, who never sinned, to be the offering for our sin, so that we could be made right with God through Christ."

Becoming the offering for someone else's sin is no easy feat. But it is perfect love and angelic sacrifice. When we do motherhood God's way, including the passageway to motherhood–childbirth!–the sacrifices make us more selfless, mature, humble, and wise. It's amazing what unconditional love will do *for* you and *to* you.

Sacrifice is not easy. If it is, then that is not a true sacrifice for you. Sacrifice costs you something, whether time, money, energy, tears, hard work–you name it! Childbirth and motherhood involve many sacrifices that ultimately make us more like Jesus (when done God's way). These sacrifices serve great purposes that refine our love to look more like God's love over time.

Again, the word "supernatural" is not synonymous with the word "easy." Even pain-free childbirth experiences often involve challenges in pregnancy or in the postpartum period, in motherhood itself, or in a combination of them all!

Nothing this valuable comes cheap. The essence of motherhood is love; and love is inseparable from sacrifice. Unconditional love does not exist without *conditions* (hardships!) that tempt you to prioritize yourself over the one you love. Love that is not tested cannot be considered unconditional because it's only been observed under one condition—the "good."

Love that remains grounded through good *and* bad conditions is unconditional love. And many of those bad conditions involve sacrifice to continue loving. For this, you must tap into the love of God which is the only perfect love. Through Jesus, we see the example of unconditional love through His ultimate sacrifice that revolutionized the world and all of eternity.

Jesus loved humankind through conditions of being adored, worshiped, and appreciated as well as conditions of being spit on, beaten, mocked, and literally crucified. Through His power, we have access to the same perfect love to stand through any sacrifice.

Sacrifices require work either outwardly, inwardly, or both. But the good news, Mama, is that we were built for this. We were made to conceive life, carry it, and to deliver babies through the birth canal that God built into our very bodies! When you are literally birthing life, your trophy at the end of the marathon—baby!—is worth infinitely more than the convenience of foregoing childbirth.

> *When you are literally birthing life, your trophy at the end of the marathon—baby!—is worth infinitely more than the convenience of foregoing childbirth.*

So, let's put in the WORK, Ladies! Don't be afraid of the challenge of childbirth. You were made to do this. You were literally designed to give birth by Almighty God. He is the Potter, and we are the clay (Isaiah 64:8); and God has physically molded our bodies to be able to give birth.

Whether you endure labor or persevere through a long c-section recovery, all types of birth require sacrifice on major levels.

By your faith and preparation plus God's grace, your birth experience might be short and pain-free or it might be long and challenging, yet peaceful and powerful. Either way, birth is always an intense, life-altering experience.

Lean into the intensity of contractions: do not fight them with tension or dread. Use the power of [25]self-talk in labor to support your work ethic the same way you would do during an intense workout:

"I can do hard things."
"I came here to WORK, not to play."
"I am excited to meet my baby."
"I welcome contractions to my body."
"My uterus is doing her job well. Praise God!"
"Bring it on!"
"For by You I can run against a troop, and by my God I can leap over a wall." Psalm 18:29 (ESV)
"I can do all things through Christ who strengthens me." Philippians 4:13 (NKJV)

---

[25] Visit www.powerfulpeacedoula.com/products to purchase the full decks of my affirmation cards and scripture cards to empower your soul for birth and give your mind beautiful, visual focal points.

7

———

Coping
With Complications–
Like a Believer!

*O*ne of my clients was experiencing a very long labor that eventually led to her obstetrician suggesting a c-section …

The obstetrician claimed that my client's pelvis was too narrow and that the baby was up too high. Because the baby was not in an ideal position, the doctor stated that my client's narrow pelvic outlet would decrease the chances that this baby would make it past the pelvic bone.

As soon as the doctor left the room, I prayed over my client and her husband, and I encouraged them. Then, the power of God filled the room! All three of us began praising God aloud, worshiping God, and speaking scriptures one after the other, rotating organically.

By the time the nurse checked my client again, the baby had turned all the way around to an occiput anterior (OA) position, ideal for delivery! Her cervix was also completely ready for the pushing stage.

Against the odds, God helped my client to push her baby out quickly and peacefully! (To read the full story, see "My Clients' Birth Stories, Part 1" in Appendix C.)

No matter the circumstance, God is able to intervene. But, we've got to be determined to ride every wave like a believer.

Some childbirth experiences are intense, but smooth, while others are both painful and rough, encountering challenges throughout pregnancy, labor, and the postpartum period. None are *easy*! Even stories of pain-free childbirth are not void of challenges. For example, labor might be pain-free, but recovery might pose a new challenge!

Now, here's a disclaimer: Labor and the postpartum period might end up feeling easier than you expected; but always remember to believe God for the best while preparing to trust Him no matter what.

Often, the challenge comes in the "test" part of the "testimony." To cope with complications like a believer, you must pray and obey through the TEST to reach the TESTimony!

See the following examples:

1. Test 1: severe nausea and vomiting in pregnancy/ Testimony 1: fully healed and eating normally
2. Test 2: threat of c-section delivery due to labor complications/ Testimony 2: successful vaginal delivery

3. Test 3: long labor/ Testimony 3: patience, endurance, peace, and joy during labor!
4. Test 4: postpartum depression/ Testimony 4: postpartum JOY
5. Test 5: high-risk for postpartum hemorrhage/ Testimony 5: bleeding is well controlled by natural oxytocin, created by God!

We serve a mighty God who can show up and do mindblowing miracles if we dare to ask and believe.

Have you ever heard the old saying "Smooth seas don't make good sailors"? To be good mothers, we need more depth in our souls to help steer our homes than the best sailors, pilots, or train operators.

It's no wonder that our very souls go through so much in childbirth–pregnancy, labor, delivery, and postpartum–, involving much more than just our bodies! I do not believe that the passageway to motherhood is easy, and I do not believe God intended for it to be easy. Life is not easy; but for those who love God and are called according to His

> "When a baby is born, so is a mother"–a new version of herself.

purpose, all things work together for our good (Romans 8:28)! Childbirth is no exception.

I often say, "When a baby is born, so is a mother"–a new version of herself. Childbirth is a beginning for a baby and a *new* beginning for a woman. My father says that hardships either make you "bitter or better," and this chapter is about how we can make the challenges of childbirth make us better.

When you birth like you believe, you can swim through the crashing waves of the sea and become a better swimmer without drowning. In other words, your soul and spirit can be strengthened through challenges in child-birth, making you a better mother, Christian, wife or career woman than you've ever been.

Labor can be a powerful training ground, building great wealth in our souls and teaching us valuable lessons that we can use for inner refinement.

Not every woman will experience health complications or labor complications, but the road to motherhood is challenging no matter the route. For some moms, the most significant challenges are found in the hormonal shifts, emotional roller coasters, or body changes.

When you engage your faith and let down your anchor in God, any and all of these challenges will make you better at some point—wiser, less vain, more mature, or stronger. Endured God's way, difficulties can mold you to be unshakeable by the things that once unnerved you. Keep in mind that some believers feel this improvement immediately while others experience it through a process.

Particularly where birth trauma is present, a mother might experience a more sensitive, easily irritable, or sad version of herself until she receives the fullness of her healing. But when she is a believer and she's fully surrendered to God, we know that, in the fullness of time, all things—even birth trauma—will work together for her good (Romans 8:28). And she WILL become a better version of herself. She will likely find herself being used by God to help others heal from trauma, too.

Our God is masterful at using pain for purpose and not allowing our suffering to be in vain! Jesus is skilled

> *Jesus is skilled both at turning obstacles into opportunities and removing obstacles altogether.*

both at turning obstacles into opportunities and removing obstacles altogether.

When complications arise in childbirth, God can intervene with a miracle! In these times when we employ our faith, we can have a much more powerful **test**imony following childbirth because of the **test** we endured. Without a test, your testimony does not exist. Childbirth itself feels like a test sometimes! When we birth God's way, we can have a beautiful testimony of supernatural childbirth.

However, not all believing mothers experience *natural* childbirth. [26]It is possible to have a supernatural childbirth without experiencing natural childbirth. Medicated birth, instrument-assisted delivery, and cesarean section delivery can all be experienced as supernatural childbirth when God says so.

God knows when a c-section delivery is safest for a baby and/or mom. God knows which scenarios medication and anesthesia are blessings for His daughters. And God can use doctors' hands to safely facilitate an instrument-assisted delivery (vacuum/forceps). With one touch from God, a mom can experience zero adverse side effects of any of these medical interventions, or experience rapid healing from any of the aggravating side effects.

My mother experienced a supernatural c-section birth that included zero surgical complications and zero adverse side effects of the surgery and medication. Her recovery was miraculously accelerated as well. In fact, she claims that her recovery was *easy*! This was her fourth birth experience, and the rest were vaginal deliveries.

---

[26] See "My Clients' Birth Stories, Part 2"in Appendix D to read testimonies of supernatural childbirth under unsuspecting circumstances.

Instead of fear, God filled her with peace and joy during the surgery and postpartum!

God is sovereign and almighty, and He specializes in bringing a message from mess, beauty from ashes, joy from sorrow, ministry from misery, and even making light shine brighter on a dark backdrop. There are no limits to God's power–the one and only true and living God.

In order to experience God's power in an unideal situation, there must be faith present. Sometimes, it's your own faith; and sometimes it's someone else's faith extended on your behalf (See Luke 5:17-25 where men lowered their paralyzed friend through the roof to be healed by Jesus. And because of their faith on the paralytic's behalf, Jesus healed him!). But, the best scenario is *both*–your faith combined with the faith of another.

Matthew 18:19-20 (ESV)
"Again I say to you, if two of you agree on earth about anything they ask, it will be done for them by my Father in heaven. For where two or three are gathered in my name, there am I among them."

During pregnancy, designate a prayer partner whose faith you trust. With this person, share what you're believing God for concerning your childbirth specifically. If that person laughs or exhibits doubt of any kind, find someone different. Pray together in preparation for labor, and consider doing this once a week.

As I've previously stated, God is not a genie in a bottle; thus He is not obligated to answer every prayer with a "yes." However, He is a good Father and loves giving good gifts to His children, especially when it is aligned with His will. God loves babies, mothers, and His own design for childbirth!

If, after you have prepared the best you can physically, spiritually, and educationally, you feel like God answered some of your prayers with a "no" in childbirth, look for the prayers that He answered with a "yes." When you seek, you will find! (See Matthew 7:7)

In my first pregnancy, I was filled with joy and excitement about the baby growing inside of me, and, overall, my pregnancy was very smooth. I did, however, experience moderate food aversions in the first trimester, along with severe hunger throughout the whole pregnancy.

My hunger was so extreme that I felt the need to eat every two hours or less! And for me, the consequence of eating too infrequently was a near-fainting experience. I'd feel dizzy, lightheaded, and eventually my vision would get blurry and my hearing dull.

The only solution was food! I could eat a footlong sub sandwich, lie down for a nap, and be woken up by hunger pains forty-five minutes after eating! Even my doctor told me that the level of hunger I was experiencing was unusual.

It was intense to say the least. These sensations drained my energy and forced me to travel with a lunchbox everywhere I went. But, my testimony is that my pregnancy remained perfectly healthy; I maintained peace and bliss every day; and I never once actually fainted!

I had prayed many times that I would not faint, and even though I experienced near-fainting experiences multiple times per week for almost ten months, I never once fainted. Oh, the goodness and mercy of God!

When I reminisce on that pregnancy, the dominant memories are joyful. Even with the difficult moments, I felt like my pregnancy was as close to perfect as it could be! God has mighty ways of making our joy full in Him when we invite Him into every area of our lives. Always remember that there is no challenge, big or small, that God cannot overcome!

I was also delivered from a fear of needles during my first pregnancy. Through a process of prayer, trusting God, and facing several tests, God set me free! Immunizations and blood draws no longer had power to frighten me and make me feel powerless.

And my final test with needles came when my labia needed minor stitching immediately following birth: What once would've had me terrified and in tears, now faded to the background of the bundle of love I was holding in my arms! I felt no pain, just slight discomfort and overwhelming gratitude! My heart overflowed with joy, love, and pride for my baby girl. This moment proved once and for all that my fear of needles was replaced by peace in God. I still carry that peace five years later as I write this book forever changed.

In my second pregnancy, I experienced a low-lying placenta. Doctors told me that, if it did not move, I would have to have a c-section delivery. The position of my placenta close to my cervix was causing bleeding during lower-body workouts, during sex, and during kegel exercises. The first time this bleeding began, I had to fight the fear of miscarriage as blood streamed down my legs in the shower!

Through prayer, faith, and the power of God's Word, I maintained my peace. I clung to my hope in Jesus all the way until receiving the report from the doctor that my placenta had moved completely to the exact position for which I had prayed!

(I had prayed that God would move my placenta to the

back of my uterus [posterior position] so my placenta would not prevent me from feeling my baby's movements like what can sometimes happen with an anterior positioned placenta.)

In my first labor experience, I labored for so long at the hospital that the doctor told me, "We should not have allowed you to labor here this long. Even though you and the baby are doing fine, hospital policy says that we have to intervene at this point. I can either break your water, give you Pitocin, or you can go home."

Contractions were so intense by this point that the sarcasm of "you can go home" felt cruel, yet my soul was not shaken. While tired and still engulfed in my labor zone mentally, emotionally, and spiritually, I casually answered the obstetrician, "Well, I guess if I have to choose one, you can break my water."

My mother immediately interrupted asking, "Kirstie, that's not what you wanted, right?" Then, she proceeded to distract the doctor saying she was going to make a phone call to a superior for a second opinion. This bought me some time!

(Tip: Carefully select the people who will support you in labor because pivotal moments can be transformed by their influence, whether for better or worse. While you're consumed in "labor land," you need trustworthy support.)

Meanwhile, my husband asked me what I wanted to do. Just minutes later, my mother asked me the same question. My response was identical to both of them: "I know God has heard my prayers, and I believe He can dilate me to 10 cm and break my water; and He can do it quickly."

Kyle and I prayed, my mom and I prayed, and my sister Neiel sent a written prayer via text message that my mother read aloud to me. As she read the prayer, my water broke. Within 30 minutes, I had dilated from 5 or 6 cm to 9 cm, and the doctor was shocked! She exclaimed, "Wow, well, if you can progress to 9 cm that fast on your own, I'll come back in 30 more minutes and see where you are then!"

Ten to fifteen minutes from that time, I felt the overwhelming sensation to push ... And the rest of the story you can read in "My Birth Stories," Appendix A.

God answered my prayer for a short, pain-free labor with a "no." Yet, He showed up with miraculous progress when I needed it. Truly, He responded to faith and prayer!

If you feel like God has answered some of your prayers during pregnancy with a "no," do not succumb to the temptation to be discouraged, Daughter of God. Keep knocking and keep asking! Knocking involves repetition, so be patient for the process, trust God, and use God's Word to sharpen your faith:

Matthew 7:7-8 (ESV)
"Ask, and it will be given to you; seek, and you will find; knock, and it will be opened to you. For everyone who asks receives, and the one who seeks finds, and to the one who knocks it will be opened."

Keep praying, keep asking, and keep believing! Sometimes, moms will reminisce on their birth experiences and feel immediate joy and gratitude, while others must dig for the treasure to discover what God hid for them–for growth, development, and beautiful change. If you experience birth trauma or complications that are hard to cope with, I challenge you to dig for the treasure like you know what kind of God we serve.

Hint: Your baby is the biggest treasure in your birth

experience, but not the *only* treasure. Dig for it like you believe that all things work together for your good because of who you are in Christ. Trust God even while you're still digging, and don't stop digging until you find the treasure. This treasure is a keepsake for your life worth cherishing.

8

Infertility

nfertility is a giant of a topic, and its prevalence and soul-stirring impact mandates attention. Human nature always wants to understand the "why" behind life circumstances that feel like tragedies. Although we will never know everything as finite human beings, God can lead us to healing if we allow Him to do that. Read the thoughts of a woman of God wrestling with infertility approaching age 40, healed in her heart and resting in faith:

> *I felt confused because I am a child of God so this could not possibly be the case for me ... I was diagnosed with a condition that meant only half of my*

reproductive system was functional. I was angry and appalled, and I was sad. I went through seasons of bitterness because I wondered why He made my body this way. God had to walk me through a process ensuring that my desire for a child did not outweigh my desire for Him. Wherever I was in the process, God was very present, sending me a song or a rainbow or speaking through a person at just the right time. Because the assurance of His presence was so strong, I got the strength to keep on. Every time I laid down my hope, He restored it somehow. The enemy wanted me to think I was not enough and that I'm not even fully a woman. God let me know that I am enough and that having a child was not my all-encompassing destiny. There are other things that need my attention, too. I faithfully reminded myself that I am fearfully and wonderfully made and that, because I have not had a child, I am not less of a woman.

–Khrystal Stanley

Wow, this woman of God truly allowed the Lord to heal her heart and fill her with joy and peace as she pursued purpose and held onto her faith and identity in Christ. Some resort to depression as a default mode of the heart under the same circumstances; but, as believers, we know there's always a better way.

Some conceive easily while others have long, discouraging waiting periods for conception. And for some, they conceive quickly but struggle to carry a pregnancy to term. Some women's conception appears to be natural while others' is nothing short of a miracle!

If infertility or miscarriage has touched your life, I extend my sincerest condolences, Sister. I do not downplay the pain in such a journey, and I pray God's speedy healing for your heart and body in Jesus' name.

If you're in a waiting period, may the peace of God cover your soul and may great FAITH arise in you, whether God's will includes biological fertility, spiritual fertility, or both.

God can do anything, and there are no limits to His power! In Aldrika Boyle's book, *Let There Be Life (Volume I)*, we see a clear example of the power of God against infertility:

> *After a year of being off birth control, I had difficulty conceiving ... To get pregnant, we took various tests and fertility drugs ... Everything we tried didn't work ... On January 23, 1995, the doctor's report read: a black female, 26 years old, with multiple cysts, tumors, and infection, must have a hysterectomy. That was one of the scariest days of my life. The desire to become a mother seemed unlikely and became lost in my heart. I was so sick I couldn't walk ... (Boyle 5).*

After a powerful journey of faith, scripture meditation and recitation, praise, shouting, tears, prayers, accountability partners, spiritual warfare, and anointing oil, Aldrika Boyle was suddenly healed! All of her pain stopped instantaneously; she could walk again; and her next doctor's report confirmed that her tumors and cysts had disappeared.

Two months later, she was pregnant. Without any trace

of morning sickness, her pregnancy flowed in the supernatural power of God with perfect health, joy, and
rejoicing (Boyle 15). Her baby was born on the anniversary
of the day her doctors determined that she needed a
hysterectomy (Boyle 16)[27]!

> *Infertility is a
> sensitive topic, but
> not even barrenness
> is out of God's
> territory to
> transform.*

Wow, what a powerful
testimony! If you are wrestling
with infertility of any kind, I
encourage you to read *Let There
Be Life (Volume I)* by Aldrika
Boyle. It's a short, easy read
that is potent and inspiring,
truly food for the soul!

Infertility is a sensitive topic,
but not even barrenness is out
of God's territory to transform. When we find written
blessings in the Bible, blessings of the womb are listed!

Genesis 49:25 (NLT)
"May the God of your father help you; may the
Almighty bless you with the blessings of the heavens
above, and blessings of the watery depths below, and
blessings of the breasts and womb."

When God told mankind to be fruitful and multiply
and replenish the earth (Genesis 1:28), He also made pro-
vision for us in the scenarios when the fulfillment of this
would be challenging.

We don't know all the reasons that infertility is so
prevalent, but we can certainly identify some factors:
genetically modified foods (seedless crops affecting
mankind's seed!), environmental toxins, pesticides in our

---

[27] Boyle, Aldrika. *Let There Be Life: Faith Over Fear, Volume I.* Wade
Christian Publishing LLC ,2022.

foods, harmful radiation from technology (cell phones, laptops, etc. reducing sperm counts) and sedentary lifestyles (degraded fitness affecting health). Along with other elements, these issues play significant roles in infertility, which then can alter genetic factors in the individual's body and/or bloodline.

Regardless of the reasons, we know that our God is powerful and there is nothing impossible for Him. Even when doctors declare people infertile, God has the power to make her/him reproduce by His blood. He is Creator God! When He speaks, new life is formed!

> *When He speaks, new life is formed!*

Matthew 17:19-21 (ESV)

[Jesus speaking] "... For truly, I say to you, if you have faith like a grain of mustard seed, you will say to this mountain, 'Move from here to there,' and it will move, and nothing will be impossible for you."

With faith, the limits are removed from our lives! There are plenty of women who have experienced the miraculous power of God opening their wombs and bringing forth new life. God is the giver of every good and perfect gift (James 1:17), and since the Bible calls children gifts (Psalm 127:3 NLT), God can make parents out of infertile people.

Just think about how God made Sarah a mother at 90 years old and Abraham a father at 100 years old! What is impossible for God? Nothing! It doesn't matter what the doctors say or what other people think about your condition.

A faithful woman of God wrestled with infertility for three years before God blessed her with pregnancy. When describing her journey, she explained the following:

The first time I heard the term "infertile," it felt like "no hope," and I didn't understand it. For me, it was a spiritual thing. I had not heard "infertility" from God, just from the doctor. In my process, I worked hard to prevent that noise from getting in the way of what God was asking me to do to get to the promise. I couldn't allow man's words to hinder God's blessing for me. My husband was overly supportive and kept the faith when I didn't have any. He led me to let go of control and be patient and keep believing. I had to let go of my timeframe and listen to my spouse who coached me along the way.

I also had many people to prophesy to me, some who identified as prophets and others who simply allowed God to speak through them, like my sister. These people told me that I would have a child and become a mother. And I also heard God speak to me after a conversation with my doctor, saying, 'Your time is coming.' I met others along the journey who were also believing God for a child, and that community helped a lot. As I waited for the promise, I was sustained by the voice of God and the faith in my husband as well as others in my community. And without medical interventions, I became pregnant!

–Denise Reynolds

God is awesome! If you're wrestling with infertility, notice three key factors in this story:

1. Faith partner(s)
2. Listening for God's voice
3. Submission

Faith partners: When this woman's faith became weak, her husband's faith remained strong. His faith served to strengthen her faith and to uplift their prayer request to God steadfastly, even in the presence of doubt. If your spouse's faith is weak, identify another faith partner.

Listening for God's voice: If Denise had listened only to the voices of doctors, she would have missed what God had in His perfect will for her. If God has plans for biological reproduction in your body, He can inform you. You cannot stand in faith on a promise you do not know you have. Only by listening for God's voice can you claim a blessing for your life. You can listen for His voice through His written Word and through His spoken word. (Keep reading: you will find scriptures that reveal God's heart concerning children.) God can speak to you directly or through others, through dreams, visions, sermons, Scripture, and the list goes on and on! Drown the voices of the media, doctors' reports, and nay-sayers and pay attention to the voice of God.

> *You cannot stand in faith on a promise you do not know you have.*

Submission: Notice in the above story how Denise's husband led her to relinquish control, have faith, and be patient. There are built-in blessings for submission to God-given authority in our lives. (See Ephesians 5:22-24 for God's thoughts about submission in marriage.) Doing things our own way will always limit our lives to our own wisdom. You can remove the limits from your life when you submit your life to the wisdom of authority figures in your life.

And oh, what sweet fruit that is produced from obedience and submission to God! For Denise, as well as for some others, the reward is motherhood. (Disclaimer: Although this woman's story did not involve medical interventions for conception, each woman should consult God for His leading as it relates to routes for conception.)

Psalm 113:9 (ESV)
"He gives the barren woman a home, making her the joyous mother of children. Praise the LORD!"

Wow, what hope to remember that God has the power to give a barren woman a child and make her a joyful mother! Our God is powerful, and there are no limits to His power. Remember this: The virgin Mary experienced immaculate conception, developing a biological pregnancy from a spiritual encounter with the Holy Spirit. Is there anything too hard for our God (Jeremiah 32:27b)? Absolutely not, Sis!

Isaiah 54:1 (NLT)
"'Sing, O childless woman, you who have never given birth! Break into loud and joyful song, O Jerusalem, you who have never been in labor. For the desolate woman now has more children than the woman who lives with her husband,' says the LORD."

Praise God and rejoice now as an expression of your faith in God! Praise Him, even when you don't feel a biological pregnancy just yet. Seek first the Kingdom of God and His righteousness and all these things will be added to you (Matthew 6:33). Be determined to be so intimate with the Holy Spirit that you conceive spiritually, becoming spiritually pregnant before you ask for a physical pregnancy.

Make sure you have spiritual fertility before physical fertility! Make your soul delight in the Lord and His presence so much that you crave Him more than the gift(s) you're requesting from Him. And as you create a covenant with God and operate in a lifestyle of obedience to God, you can begin to claim the promises of God that He made toward His covenant people– the nation of Israel.

> *Make sure you have spiritual fertility before physical fertility!*

If you're wrestling with infertility, then you will want to claim the word spoken to the nation of Israel in Deuteronomy 7:14 (NKJV): "You shall be blessed above all peoples; there shall not be a male or female barren among you or among your livestock."

Now, let's add faith and works to this thing! Do what you know to do! Do your best to rid your body of processed foods, genetically modified organisms, pesticides, and environmental toxins (lotion, body wash, laundry detergent, etc.). Focus on whole foods–organic, non-gmo fruits, vegetables, and protein sources free of hormones and antibiotics. Exercise regularly, making your temple a healthy place for a baby to grow! And remember, the health of your spouse is equally important for conception because there are wildly rising rates of infertility in males.

You may also want to see a fertility specialist with your spouse, learn, and apply that knowledge to your life.

Simultaneously, build your faith! Faith comes by hearing, and hearing by the Word of God! (Romans 10:17)

1. Meditate on scriptures that build your faith for conception.
   a. You can start with the verses in this chapter!

2. Expose yourself to testimonies of other women who have supernaturally conceived.
    a. Women in Scripture
        i. Sarah, Isaac's mom: Genesis 16:2 & Gen. 21:1-7
        ii. Hannah, Samuel's mom: 1 Samuel 1:6-20
        iii. Rebekah, Jacob & Esau's mom: Genesis 25:21
        iv. Rachel, Joseph's mom: Genesis 29:31-32 & Gen. 30:1, 22-24
        v. The unnamed wife of Manoah, Samson's mom: Judges 13:2-5, 24
        vi. The Shunammite woman: 2 Kings 4:14-17
        vii. Elizabeth, John the Baptist's mom: Luke 1:5-7, 11-15, 24-25
    b. Women you meet in-person
    c. Autobiography books
    d. Testimonies on social platforms: women on social media and podcasts with the faith you desire
3. Pray for a greater measure of faith!
4. Listen to God and write what He tells you.

As you read the stories of barren women in Scripture who received children from the Lord, notice the patience and persistence in many of these testimonies. The wait is not usually easy, but it is absolutely worth it! Ask God to ripen the fruit of patience in your life, a very important fruit of the Holy Spirit that will enrich other areas of your life as well. God's timing is often different from our timing, but His ways are perfect and He makes no mistakes.

Genesis 25:21 (NLT)
"Isaac pleaded with the LORD on behalf of his wife,
because she was unable to have children. The LORD
answered Isaac's prayer, and Rebekah became pregnant
with twins."

As you see in this scripture, God can honor the prayers and faith of another person on your behalf. Just like with any other healing, sometimes the faith of the person praying for you is stronger than your own faith, and God honors FAITH and His Word, period.

Right now, I pray for you, Sister, extending my faith even if your hurtful, discouraging journey has weakened your faith. I know that, if it is in God's will to make you a biological mother, He can do that in response to faith and prayer, even of someone else.

Father God, in the name of Jesus, I ask that you will open the womb of any barren woman reading these words and bless her with a healthy biological child within marriage. May this child bring You great glory from conception to his/her final breath and bring the parents much joy. In Jesus' name, amen.

Hebrews 11:11(NLT)
"It was by faith that even Sarah was able to have a
child, though she was barren and was too old. She
believed that God would keep his promise."

If you are suffering from infertility, I encourage you to extend *your* faith, like Sarah, and pray the prayer below from your heart:

*Heavenly Father, in the name of Jesus, I ask that
You touch my reproductive system with Your
almighty power and give me a biological child.*

Please heal my body and reverse any damaging effects of food or fluids that I've ingested, or any toxins or radiation that has harmed my body or bodily functions. Please heal me completely! Right now, I renounce spirits of barrenness and release any spiritual roots of barrenness in my life. By Jesus' blood, I break any curse off my life.

Lord, please bless me with a healthy, biological child; a healthy, smooth pregnancy; a peaceful, time-efficient labor and delivery; and a joyful, healthy postpartum period.

And lastly, but not least, I pray that God will stir spiritual fertility in you, greater than you've ever experienced. May you love God in richer ways, desiring Him more than anyone or anything. And may you dare to believe God for big requests, like you know how powerful your Father is. In Jesus' name, amen.

9

Miscarriage

*T*he pain of loss like miscarriage can feel like you're going through fire: feeling burned by life and suffocating in the smoke. But if you go through the fire God's way, He will be in the fire with you as He was with Shadrach, Meshach and Abednego in the book of Daniel chapter three. Those on the outside noticed that these three Hebrew boys were not alone because there was a fourth man in the fire ... Jesus had appeared!

God always has been with His people in the fire, and He still is. See this testimony from a woman of God who endured two miscarriages:

> *It's something when you have one, but when you*

have a second one after that, you think, "Is something wrong with me? Will I ever have any children?" I fell into depression. Because I did not want to start blaming God, I told myself that the enemy comes to steal, kill, and destroy. I read scriptures often, just a little at a time while depressed ... I allowed myself to feel it, not rush the process. I allowed myself to grieve. Friends continued to pray for me, and I know that helped me heal. My healing was completed at a conference I attended. A lady hugged me, and I melted and heard the Lord say, "Her arms are an extension of My arms." I laughed in the Holy Spirit and then saw a vision of angels around me. When I went back to church after that, someone told me I looked different, like I was glowing, lighter and brighter! It was the supernatural power of God, prayer, and pressing into what God had already shown me and my husband and what He had already told us. I had my fire back and my faith back.

–Anonymous

Daughter of God, if you've experienced a miscarriage, I extend my sincerest condolences. There are few words to adequately describe the deep sentiments of loss, disappointment, and grief that accompany miscarriage. God sees you, knows even your unspoken sorrows, and He feels you to the depths of your soul.

Psalm 56:8 (NLT)

"You keep track of all my sorrows. You have collected all my tears in your bottle. You have recorded each one in your book."

Your pain is not unnoticed by God. And the Almighty Comforter wants to comfort your soul in ways that no human can do. Some things bear such weight in your soul that you need supernatural comfort, and that is available to every believer in Jesus Christ.

2 Corinthians 1:3-5 (ESV)
"Blessed be the God and Father of our Lord Jesus Christ, the Father of mercies and God of all comfort, who comforts us in all our affliction, so that we may be able to comfort those who are in any affliction, with the comfort with which we ourselves are comforted by God. For as we share abundantly in Christ's sufferings, so through Christ we share abundantly in comfort too."

Since God is the giver of life, let's take a look at what His Word says about miscarriage in Exodus 23:25-26 (NKJV): "So you shall serve the LORD your God, and He will bless your bread and your water. And I will take sickness away from the midst of you. No one shall suffer miscarriage or be barren in your land; I will fulfill the number of your days."

This word spoken towards the children of Israel pertains to the people of God in general, as Israel is a picture of Christ's church. Now, as we look at the promises of God, we must remember a few things:

1. Promises of God are accompanied by qualifications.
2. Faith activates promises of God in your life.
3. You must work the Word in your own mind and heart for the Word to work for you.

Let's look at an example of number one in John 15:14-15 (NKJV):

"You are My friends if you do whatever I command you. No longer do I call you servants, for a servant does not know what his master is doing; but I have called you friends, for all things that I heard from My Father I have made known to you."

These verses do not indicate that everyone is Jesus' friend automatically nor do they indicate that He will share His secrets with people without prerequisites. Rather, the Word says that you are Jesus' friends IF you do what He commands you to do. God requires obedience for His friendship and secrets.

Now, as we discuss promises like "no one shall suffer miscarriage in your land," in Exodus 23:26, let's back it up in Exodus 23 to the verses that came before this one:

"But if you indeed **obey** His voice and do all that I speak, then I will be an enemy to your enemies and an adversary to your adversaries. You shall not bow down to their gods, nor serve them, nor do according to their works; but you shall utterly overthrow them and completely break down their sacred pillars."

And again, we read of OBEDIENCE before attaining the promise. We again read the words "IF" you _____, "THEN, I will _____."

Sometimes the power of testimonies paints messages clearer, showing us the truth of God's Word applied in real life scenarios. Read below the story of a devoted woman of God who experienced two miscarriages herself and learned powerful revelation from God through the pain:

Sudden loss ... no preparation for it. It was unexpected. One day you go to the doctor and everything's healthy, and the next week there's no heartbeat. As the Bible says, "Hope deferred makes the heart sick" (Proverbs 13:12a NKJV). The hopes and dreams I had for this child and life with this child died suddenly. After I cried and went through the mourning and came back to some level of normalcy, I heard God repeatedly telling me through various sources that I needed to adopt a vegan lifestyle. Through God's truth, I knew that I could not get to my proverbial promised land without committing to a vegan diet.

I had tumors and cysts in my body, and the baby could not dwell there. My temple [body] was not sustainable for life to grow. I heard God say, "Maggie, if you are not obedient and don't submit to Me, then healing and conception won't happen." He showed me that on the other side of obedience was complete healing for my body and reproductive organs, removal of tumors and cysts, and then carrying a pregnancy. Faith and works! I didn't want to be a vegan. I fought it, but God showed me that I was sick and miscarried because of the state of my temple. When I changed my diet in obedience to God, I found less depression, fogginess [of mind], and sickness.

I was healed on the inside and outside! Six months after becoming a vegan, doctors could not find the cysts or tumors. Unfortunately, after the healing, I decided to partially follow the vegan diet. I thought that God would still bless me if I committed to being a vegan four days a week and enjoyed meat the other three days. But the truth of the matter was that I was still disobedient. Not too long after that, I experienced a second miscarriage. God said to me, "Partial obedience is still disobedience." After this, I went back to a fully vegan diet and conceived and carried full term. Even outside of childbirth, disobedience hinders the growth of godly seeds. God healed my womb, and that's how I was able to carry Micah.

–Magalie Awosika

Wow, what a clear picture of the blessings of obedience! Sister, search your heart and ask the Lord if there's anything you need to surrender in obedience to Him. This testimony is not to convince you that adopting a vegan lifestyle will lead to a healthy pregnancy; but rather, this story is to show you the power of obedience to whatever God requires of you. Ask God to search your heart and point out any idolatry (anything that has priority in your heart above God), bitterness, or unforgiveness. Then ask Him to help you live with greater obedience even in your heart.

Remember, the Bible assures us that God's grace is sufficient for us and that His strength is made perfect in our weakness (2 Corinthians 12:9). God does NOT require perfection from us, but He does require obedience and faithful repentance.

When you are believing God to heal your heart and body from miscarriage and to give you another baby to carry full term, MEDITATE on His Word. When I say "work the Word," I mean that you exercise your faith by repetition of scriptures pertaining to miscarriage, healing, and fertility.

Faith comes by hearing, and hearing by the Word of God (Romans 10:17). Read the scriptures, repeat the scriptures, think about God's words consistently, and expose yourself to testimonies of other women who have birthed babies after miscarriage.

These practices will strengthen your faith and work the Word in your life. Meditating on God's Word takes His promises from being "words on a page" to becoming your story. When the Word is IN you, your faith is activated towards the promise. Faith requires us to believe the promise *before* we see it!

If you believe that YOU are included among the people of God described in Exodus 23:26, you know that your next pregnancy does not have to end in miscarriage. Use the Word to cast out fear of a repeated miscarriage! Why? Because 2 Timothy 1:7 assures us that fear does not come from God, but instead God grants us power, love, and a sound mind.

2 Timothy 1:7 (NKJV)
"For God has not given us a spirit of fear, but of power and of love and of a sound mind."

Daughter of God, REPEAT this scripture until you feel it in your soul.

On another note, while faith and obedience are very important to an abundant life, bad things do not always happen as a consequence of sin. This means that obedience and repentance will not guarantee exemption from sufferings like miscarriage.

The book of Job proves to us that sin is not always the reason we experience tragedy, loss, or grief. As one of the most righteous men who ever lived, Job lost his children, his wealth, and his health.

As much as we want to believe that righteousness alone will prevent bad things from happening, that has not been true throughout history and still is false.

Another truth that the story of Job (and similar stories) reveal is that God cares more about our development than our comfort. God does not do bad things; but He will sometimes allow bad things to happen for the greater good.

Also, He will restore what's been lost when you remain faithful. Even if it's not in His will to restore babies biologically, He will restore your soul in greater ways than you could imagine.

I believe something about hardships that my father taught me many years ago: "Everything is either God-sent or God-used."

Since the Bible says that children are a gift from the Lord, we know that it's not in God's perfect will for miscarriage to happen. But, when it does happen, God is more than able to use that loss for His glory and for your good. Who knows the healing that would flow to you and through you to other families after what you would have endured …?

Through loss of any kind, God is able to comfort you, strengthen you, and make you a master comforter to others. He can build compassion, empathy, and mercy through what feels like tragedy and form the best version of you through the pain.

God does not promise us that we will never suffer; but He does promise His people that He will never leave us nor forsake us (Hebrews 13:5). When you invite God into the dark, sorrowful places, He will heal you so deeply that others will be amazed by how you emerge from darkness into light.

God can use tragedy, loss, and grief to make you more mature spiritually and emotionally, to purify your heart, to make you more resilient than you thought possible, more compassionate and empathetic, wiser, and the list goes on!

Not only that, but God can help you emerge from those situations without any evidence of the darkness you've been through. You can exit tragedy with only the sweet fruit of what He's developed in you and through you that will inspire and encourage others! In Daniel chapter three, we read that these Hebrew men came out of the fiery furnace, not only alive, but all of their hair was intact, clothes not burned, and they didn't even *smell* like smoke!

Daniel 3:27 (ESV)
"And the satraps, the prefects, the governors, and the king's counselors gathered together and saw that the fire had not had any power over the bodies of those men. The hair of their heads was not singed, their cloaks were not harmed, and no smell of fire had come upon them."

What a miracle! We know the furnace was blazing hot and scary, yet God's presence set miracles in motion. I'm sure at some point they wondered, "Why hasn't God delivered us from this yet and stopped them from being able to throw us into the fire? He can do anything, so why not save us from going in?!"

Remember, the Scripture records in Daniel 3:19 that King Nebuchadnezzar ordered that the fiery furnace be heated seven times hotter than usual, which killed the men who threw Shadrach, Meshach, and Abednego into the fire!

The truth is, God *did* deliver them from the fiery furnace. In our human nature, we naturally want God to answer our prayers in the most comfortable way possible. In this case, the most comfortable form of deliverance would have been sparing them from entering the fiery furnace.

To the contrary, God answered in a way that tempted them to fear and doubt but then made them stronger and more faith-filled than they were before! They left with a greater testimony than they would have, had they not entered the fire. Shadrach, Meshach, and Abednego were not delivered from the test, but they were empowered to *pass* the test! They also won other souls to the saving power of Christ as others witnessed the miracle that emerged from the fire! This same phenomenon happens with the people of God modern-day when we remain faithful to God. It's always bigger than us …

Human nature typically wants to know *why* the tragedy happens. In the "why," we often feel like we gain closure and/or comfort. But just like we want our children to trust us even when they don't understand, God desires the same.

> The mysteries of God challenge our level of trust.

The mysteries of God challenge our level of trust. Sometimes He will make it clear to us why certain situations happened; and we feel comforted when we can understand the reasons. However, as finite human beings, we are not all-knowing beings: we will never know everything or the reason for everything.

1 Corinthians 2:16 (NLT)
"For who can know the Lord's thoughts? Who knows enough to teach Him? …"

As much as our human nature wants to know God's thoughts asking "Why?" "Why me?" or "When will it end?", we will not always know these answers, and definitely not in our ideal timing.

Isaiah 55:8-9 (ESV)
"For my thoughts are not your thoughts, neither are your ways my ways, declares the LORD. For as the heavens are higher than the earth, so are my ways higher than your ways and my thoughts than your thoughts."

When we trust the sovereignty of God, the mysteries become easier for our souls to accept.

We must trust that we serve the all-wise God who makes no mistakes and always has plans to prosper us, never to harm us (Jeremiah 29:11).

And let's not forget: Everyone–Christian or not–will experience pain and sorrows in life. Both believers and non-believers suffer through miscarriage(s). But I would much rather endure as a faithful servant of Christ with all of His supernatural help than to go through grief without the Comforter of my soul when human help fails.

If you have experienced miscarriage(s) and are still hoping for a successful pregnancy, pray this prayer:

> *Heavenly Father, in the name of Jesus, I ask that You please heal my heart from all emotional wounds, protect my heart from all impurity, and fill my soul with life-transforming FAITH. Give me faith to trust You whether Your perfect will for me includes a biological pregnancy, a spiritual pregnancy, or both. Please heal my reproductive system and give me wisdom as I take care of my*

body. I ask that You please bless me with a biological child in Your perfect timing. Help my body carry that baby full term in perfect health and wholeness for me and the baby. Bless me with a peaceful, smooth, time-efficient labor, delivery, and postpartum recovery. Thank You, Giver of Life, Creator God! For I know that with You, all things are possible. In Jesus' mighty name, amen.

10

How to Pray Prayers God Hears

Psalm 66:18 (NLT) "If I had not confessed the sin in my heart, the Lord would not have listened."

Wow, you mean to tell me that God does not always listen to our prayers?! Yes, that is correct. It is important to heed God's Word to understand what can hinder our prayers so that we can remove the obstacles. God wants us to have fruitful prayer lives, and that's precisely why He teaches us how to do so.

As we read in Psalm 66:18, it is important to confess our sins to God. In some cases, it is also necessary to confess our sins to a person that we may have offended.

The Bible even tells husbands that their prayers will be hindered if they do not treat their wives as the Word instructs (1 Peter 3:7).

Before we move forward, I want to give you a heads up that this chapter is filled with scriptures! It's important for you to see what the Word says about the prayers that will and will not be answered, and how to pray. This is not based on opinion, but on the only real standard for truth–the Bible. So let's talk about it!

Take heed to God's Word in total obedience before expecting God to do miracles in your life or answer big prayers for you. Indeed, God does answer "yes" to prayers when we do not deserve it, but it's in your best interest to prepare your heart, faith, and your actions for God's best to be unleashed in your life.

In Isaiah 59:2, the Word tells us that God is powerful, not too weak to save you, but that your sins can separate you from God and cause Him to turn away and NOT listen to you.

Isaiah 59:1-2 (NLT)
"Listen! The LORD's arm is not too weak to save you, nor is his ear too deaf to hear you call. It's your sins that have cut you off from God. Because of your sins, he has turned away and will not listen anymore."

> Make sure the posture of your heart is the right posture to RECEIVE from God.

Before you ask God for big things like a living soul–a baby ... before you ask God to grant specific requests for your pregnancy, labor, and postpartum recovery ...

Search your heart, Sister. Make sure the posture of your heart is the right posture to RECEIVE from God.

We know that sins can hinder our prayers; but often we only focus on sins that we can see in obvious behavior. What about the sins of the heart that no one may see but God? For example, idolatry ...

Modern-day idols don't always look like golden calves or statues, but idols are anything that receives more attention or affection than God in your life. Some women even make an idol out of motherhood–being consumed by those desires more than their desires for God. A woman can set up her husband as an idol of her heart, her child as an idol (even an unborn child!), her career, cell phone, pornography, romance, or any number of things!

Ezekiel 14:3 (NLT)
"Son of man, these leaders have set up idols in their hearts. They have embraced things that will make them fall into sin. Why should I listen to their requests?"

We know that idolatry is serious to God because He made it clear in the Ten Commandments that "You shall have no other gods before Me" (Exodus 20:3 NKJV). And here in Ezekiel 14:3, we see that idolatry can deter God from listening to our prayer requests.

In addition to idolatry, sins of the heart could be jealousy, envy, judgment, pride, self-righteousness, and the list goes on. When you pray, ask the Holy Spirit to show you if there are any sins, whether obvious or hidden, that you need to renounce.

Scripture shows us what lifestyles, attitudes, and heart postures lead to more answered prayers. Since getting answers is our goal when we pray, we should heed the Bible!

1 John 3:21-22 (ESV)
"Beloved, if our heart does not condemn us, we have confidence before God; and whatever we ask we receive

from him, because we keep his commandments and do what pleases him."

Keeping God's commandments and doing what pleases Him–this is obedience. Disobedience blocks blessings! God does bless people who do not deserve His big gifts–who DOES?!–, but for such big requests, let's do a heart check to increase the chances of God's favor falling upon our lives in the area of childbirth.

> Disobedience blocks blessings!

Another reason for hindered prayer is wrong motives. Could it be that sometimes we want to take the easy route– avoiding inconvenience or pain that would actually strengthen us? Or could it be that we want to prove something for selfish gain? Human nature seeks pleasure, comfort, and superficial gain above development of our inward parts. In reality, God cares more about our development than our comfort. He is a good Father who sees beyond temporary pleasure to our long-term purpose.

James 4:3 (NLT)
"And even when you ask, you don't get it because your motives are all wrong—you want only what will give you pleasure."

As it relates to childbirth, good motives are children and a smooth, peaceful birth experience after God's original design. It is a good motive to want God's presence to fill your birth experience and to dwell in perfect love and safety.

Avoid ungodly motives that boost your own ego, seek attention from others, or intentionally compete with someone else. Some women desire an unmedicated birth for the motive of proving how strong they are. What about the motive of proving how strong God is? Or, they want a natural birth to paint a picture of perfection to enhance their reputation. Sometimes, the carnal motive is to birth the same way that her sister(s), mother, or admirable friend birthed their babies. As believers, we should not live in comparison to others!

Some desire pregnancy because it's the status quo for a female past a certain age. And others want to be pregnant because they desire the attention and special treatment to which it can lead! Now sisters, don't forget this one: some women want a baby to trap a man. Their goal is to obligate the man to stay with them or to provide for them financially.

Impure motives can be any number of things, but it's important to ask yourself the following question: "How will a 'yes' to my prayer request bring glory to God?" The answer to this question will help you understand whether your prayer request is carnal and selfish or aligned with the heart of God.

If you realize that your motives are ungodly, change your focus. As the Word says in Colossians 3:2, focus on things that are above, not on earthly things. And as you engulf your heart in heavenly values, ensure that your earthly affairs are honoring God. Don't just spend time praying, fasting and serving in church while neglecting your work and family responsibilities and while mistreating others. Your earthly relationships directly affect your relationship with God!

In Matthew 6:14-15, we learn that God won't forgive us if we don't forgive others. And Mark 11:25 (ESV) clearly instructs us to forgive first when we pray: "And whenever you stand praying, forgive, if you have anything against anyone, so that your Father also who is in heaven may forgive you your trespasses."

Do you really want to ask something big of God while not being forgiven by God? Reconcile yourself with anyone you are offended with and forgive whether he/she apologizes or not. In forgiveness, you will find freedom. Unforgiveness taints the heart; and you will find more answered prayers on the other side of forgiveness.

In Matthew 5:23-24, the Word tells us that, if we are presenting a sacrifice at the altar and we remember an offense we have with another person, we should leave our sacrifice at the altar and go reconcile with that person.

Prayers could be hindered because of disobedience, idolatry, wrong motives, unforgiveness, or because it's just not God's will.

1 John 5:14-15 (ESV)

"And this is the confidence that we have toward him, that if we ask anything according to his will he hears us. And if we know that he hears us in whatever we ask, we know that we have the requests that we have asked of him."

Isn't it a confidence booster to know that God promises to hear you AND fulfill your request as long as it's according to His will?! Sometimes, God answers "no" because the request is not in His will for that person's life. Other times, her timing did not match God's timing: she perceived His answer as "no" when it was actually "wait." God sometimes requires us to exercise patience while He refines us or our circumstances. God's refining prepares us for the very blessing for which we've prayed. Understand that, along with every blessing comes a corresponding challenge: And it is God's will to prepare you for that challenge so you may better receive the blessing!

Other times, we would receive more from God if we would utilize the power of confession. The Word says that, when we confess our sins and pray for each other, we can find HEALING right there! This confession requires honesty and vulnerability with God and with others. Whatever healing you may need for your reproductive system, healing for pregnancy complications, healing from past birth trauma, or just healing for your soul–it's available!

James 5:16 (ESV)
"Therefore, confess your sins to one another and pray for one another, that you may be healed. The prayer of a righteous person has great power as it is working."

Through Christ, we have mighty POWER in our prayers. When we pray, we're not asking a flawed human to do something for us; but rather, we are asking a perfect God to move on our behalf with angels at His command. When you pray, you must extend your faith, not mere empty words. Faith infuses your words with POWER!

Faith infuses your words with POWER!

Hebrews 11:6 (ESV)
"And without faith it is impossible to please him, for whoever would draw near to God must believe that he exists and that he rewards those who seek him."

I don't know about you, but it excites me to think about the rewards God gives when we seek Him! Because the Bible calls children *rewards*, they are among the blessings available to women who diligently seek God for them.

Psalm 127:3 (ESV)
"Behold, children are a heritage from the LORD, the fruit of the womb a reward."

When you decide you're going to ask something of God in faith, also ask God to remove doubt from your mind. Doubt weakens your prayers in the spirit, while faith strengthens your prayers.

James 1:6-8 (ESV)
"But let him ask in faith, with no doubting, for the one who doubts is like a wave of the sea that is driven and tossed by the wind. For that person must not suppose that he will receive anything from the Lord; he is a double-minded man, unstable in all his ways."

Scripture clearly teaches us that a lack of faith can be a reason that God answers some prayers with a "no." Even though it's human nature to doubt the things we cannot see, God is able to diminish doubt itself when we ASK! Have faith that God can do anything, including strengthening your faith. Faith is such a big deal to God that He even counts faith as righteousness, like He did with Abraham.

Abraham was not perfect enough to claim his blessings as rewards for his own goodness. What he did, however, as the Father of Faith, was extend what looked like CRAZY faith in God, no matter what anyone thought about him!

Romans 4:2-3 (ESV)
"For if Abraham was justified by works, he has something to boast about, but not before God. For what does the Scripture say? 'Abraham believed God, and it was counted to him as righteousness.'"

So feel free to ask God for big things, believing He can do it. Show God that you believe in His power by showing Him the kind of faith that might look crazy to others.

For some moms, crazy faith looks like believing God for pain-free labor and delivery. Well, He's answered that many times and continues to do so! For others, crazy faith looks like asking God for a FEAR-free birth, even when faced with haunting thoughts from a previous birth or horror stories from others. He's answered that one many times too, and continues.

For infertile women, crazy faith may look like asking God for a biological baby, regardless of what the doctors are saying about your health status. Or, it could be asking God to make spiritual fertility enough, to bring contentment with whatever His will is, or to show you who needs a mother.

Adoption, spiritual sons and daughters, biological babies, and contentment no matter what: These are all requests that can take crazy faith to pursue. But, all of these are EASY for our Heavenly Father to deliver, according to His will for your life.

When you answer God's call on your life and live a fruitful Christian life according to the Scriptures, God tells us that He will give us whatever we ask in the name of Jesus!

John 15:16 (ESV)
"You did not choose me, but I chose you and appointed you that you should go and bear fruit and that your fruit should abide, so that **whatever** you ask the Father in my name, he may give it to you."

I know it sounds simple, but it takes faith, self-discipline, and faithfulness to bear godly fruit in your life. Whether you are asking God to help you conceive, to bless you with a smooth natural childbirth, to heal you from a miscarriage, or to fill your postpartum season with joy, seek God first, above all else. Pray diligently with faith, and then watch all that you need be provided by God.

Matthew 6:33 (ESV)
"But seek first the kingdom of God and his righteousness, and all these things will be added to you."

God knows the desires of your heart. And when you surrender your heart to Him, He can place NEW desires in your heart, according to His will. Release your desires to God in the form of prayer requests and watch Him grant the desires of your heart!

Proverbs 10:24 (ESV)
"What the wicked dreads will come upon him, but the desire of the righteous will be granted."

11

The Birth Space

The birth space is a sacred space where new life is born, and often new versions of mamas are born. It is a special place that should be treated with honor, respect, and thoughtful preparation. Because childbirth is God's design, the birth space belongs to Him. But just like your body, will you dedicate it to Him as a temple for His spirit to dwell? Will you apply wisdom as you prepare your birth zone, using a strategy? Or simply "go with the flow"?

It's your choice. When you optimally prepare your birth space, you set yourself up to witness miracles in the room. In this chapter, you will learn the blueprint of *how* to practically prepare your birth space with wisdom.

The first step to seeing miracles is inviting the Miracle-Worker! But first, remember who has the power to make that decision, along with all other decisions regarding your baby and your body.

Daughter of God, *you* have authority in the birth space! The decision-maker in the room with the most authority is not your doctor, nurse, nor doula–but you, Mom.

For your birth, you have the authority to ...

1. Select **where** you will deliver your baby.
    a. Hospital
    b. Birth center
    c. Home
2. Decide **how** you plan to deliver.
    a. Medicated/unmedicated
    b. Natural/medicalized
    c. Vaginal/c-section
    d. Spontaneous labor/induced labor
    e. Water birth/bed delivery
    f. Position options
    g. And the list goes on ...
3. Exercise your **birth rights** wherever you deliver.
    a. Eating in labor
    b. Informed consent
    c. Requesting a second opinion or different medical provider
    d. And the list goes on!
4. Invite **whom** you want in the birth room.
5. Decide elements of your birth [28]atmosphere.

---

[28] See the chapter, "*How to* Birth Like You Believe, Part 2" for details on preparing your birth atmosphere.

While there is much to cover within your authority in the birth space, this chapter focuses on #4, whom you invite in the birth room. ([29]See my online childbirth education course for details about your birth rights, plus vital information on the "how" and "where" to deliver.)

It's very important to invite the right people in your birth space: medical professionals, doulas, partners, best friends, or mothers. Everyone makes an impact on your birth environment that is crucial to your experience. YOU decide who enters and who exits, if someone needs to be dismissed.

Negativity, fear, insensitivity, ignorance (about the birth process), and rudeness have no place in the birth space. Anyone who seems to subtract from the peace of your environment should be asked to leave.

When inviting friends or family members to your labor experience, select people who make you feel free, supported, and safe. Avoid inviting anyone out of obligation because this occasion is not for them: it's for you! Each member of your birth team should add to your labor experience, not attend as a spectator to make him/her feel special. Because of the hormonal nature of labor, your labor will progress best when you feel comfortable and happy, not irritated, offended, or uneasy.

Whichever family members or friends you invite to labor with you, please share with them what you are believing God for and what your birth goals are. Let them read your birth plan and pray with you in advance, helping them to get aligned with your faith for birth. If they laugh or seem doubtful, insensitive, or unwilling to learn and adapt according to your needs, replace them.

---

[29] See *Powerful Peace Birth Course* at www.powerfulpeacedoula.com.

Avoid having too many people in your birth space, when possible. Assign clear roles to each person, and once all roles have been covered, there is no need to continue expanding the guest list for your birth room. For example, your medical professionals cover any medical bases; your doula offers professional support for comfort techniques and advocacy plus other physical, educational, or emotional needs; and your primary support partner (baby's father/your mother/best friend) is your primary source of emotional comfort–the most familiar addition to your birth team and key person for oxytocin release.

You might have two members of your birth team who share the responsibility of your emotional safety blanket with each of them providing different elements. For example, your husband might serve as your primary birth space guardian, protector, and source of physical affection. Your mother or sister might be your prayer warrior and somewhat of a spiritual doula, providing continuous prayer, speaking scriptures where appropriate, and encouraging you verbally.

Invite medical professionals, a doula, and FAITH professional(s)! You need someone to sharpen your faith if it gets weak and to remind you of your faith when hormones make your mind cloudy. You need someone to pray over you and speak life to you in moments of discouragement and someone to encourage you and find the "silver lining" in anything. Sometimes a good Christian doula can also fill the role of a "faith professional," but make sure the role is covered however you can.

Remember that the most important SOMEBODY you should invite to your birth is the Holy Spirit. You have the authority to make your birth room into a sanctuary, inviting God's presence in a thick, miraculous way.

As a Christ-follower, the Holy Spirit is with you

wherever you go; however, when you intentionally invite Him into your childbirth experience, you will notice greater power! Imagine having a family member living in your house but in a bedroom of your house when an important event is occurring in the living room. Don't compartmentalize the Holy Spirit in your life, blocking off certain areas or events of your life. Invite Him into every room of the house–so to speak–in your life, including your birth experience.

> *God is perfect love, and in the fullness of His presence, fear cannot survive.*

When you command fear to leave and invite Perfect Love to fill the room in Jesus' name, it will be done. God is perfect love, and in the fullness of His presence, fear cannot survive.

You have the authority to turn your birth room into a sanctuary in the following ways:

1. Play praise and worship music that welcomes God's presence.
   o According to Psalm 22:3 (KJV), God inhabits the praises of His people.
   o Praise God, and He can fill your birth space!
2. Invite faith partners: husband/mom/best friend/Christian doula–anyone who has an intimate relationship with God and who makes you feel comfortable and safe.
   o Matthew 18:19-20 (ESV) "Again I say to you, if two of you agree on earth about anything they ask, it will be done for them by my Father in heaven. For where two or three are gathered in my name, there am I among them."

3. Remove any pagan objects: i.e. crystals, Buddha figurines, satanic symbols, New Age symbols (e.g. third eye), etc.
4. Bring anointing oil in your birth bag and anoint the doorposts, windows, bedpost or birth tub.
   o Hereby, you mark that territory for Jesus and restrict demonic spirits.
5. Set up objects that remind you of your faith.
   o Posters with scriptures and/or images of the cross
   o Bible
   o Any special prayer blanket, shawl, or handkerchief you may have
6. Meditate on scriptures in labor (notecards/posters/Bible app, etc.).
   o [30]See my scripture cards for pregnancy and birth.
7. Pray aloud.
   o You may choose to do this when your medical professionals have left the room OR not, haha!
8. Sing to God in between contractions while applicable.

When your birth room is a sanctuary, a temple for God to inhabit, there is great freedom in the air. Almighty God is there, and He has your best interests at heart. He loves you more than anyone could ever love you, and you and your baby are safe in His arms.

In God's presence, you are free from fear, anxiety, worry, and even from "bad" doctors' reports. Whose

---

[30] Visit www.powerfulpeacedoula.com/products.

report will you believe? You can choose to believe the report of the Lord and live in His peace that passes all understanding (See Philippians 4:7). In His presence, there is fullness of joy (See Psalm 16:11)!

You are not bound to anyone's horror story nor are you bound to sorrow. You are free in Jesus to experience all that He has for you! Trust Him with your heart, your body, and your precious baby.

Think and pray about who to invite into this space, and be sure to invite the One who created you and your baby. With God, all things are possible (See Matthew 19:26). He knows no limits and no boundaries. He is faithful, trustworthy, and the all-wise God.

With this good, good Father in the room, all good things are available to you, Daughter of God.

12

How to Birth
Like You Believe,
Part 1

When you birth like you believe, childbirth becomes an exciting adventure with you, God, and your unborn child. Faith and corresponding actions change everything! Miracles are in the air, new life is imminent, and a combination of peace and thrill are flooding your soul.

So many mothers never experience supernatural childbirth, not even Christians ... so *how*? What makes the difference? This chapter and the next will teach you *how to* birth like you believe.

First, hear me clearly: Faith without works is dead.

"What good is it, my brothers, if someone says he has faith but does not have works? ... So also faith by itself, if it does not have works, is dead" James 2:14a, 17 (ESV).

Prayer is not the only ingredient to a supernatural childbirth experience. The Bible makes it clear to us that we must engage both faith and works (actions!) for the outcomes we desire. Now, let's discuss *how* to birth like you believe.

(1) Expose yourself to a new outlook on childbirth, discovering the possibilities.

You've already begun step one by reading *Birth Like You Believe!* You cannot do better if you do not know what "better" looks like! With renewed perspective, you understand that there is more to childbirth than stories of fear, trauma, and suffering.

See the birth stories in Appendices A-D containing testimonies of the power of God in other women's birth stories. When you read about how God moved in the labor and birth experiences of others, your faith is quickened by examples of His glory in childbirth.

Revelation 12:11a (KJV) "And they overcame him by the blood of the Lamb, and by the **word** of their **testimony** ..."

Expose yourself to stories of supernatural childbirth experiences from other like-minded moms. Whether through YouTube, podcasts, [31]books, or in-person encounters, a [32]testimony can change your perspective and

---

[31] Book recommendation: *Supernatural Childbirth* written by Jackie Mize

[32] See Appendices A-D to read stories of other moms who experienced God's power in birth.

give you power to overcome obstacles in Jesus' name. Testimonies are beautiful fuel for your faith!

(2) Pray over your pregnancy, baby, body, labor, delivery, and postpartum recovery–daily!

When you form this kind of prayer habit, you can be confident that your pregnancy and childbirth experience are COVERED in prayer. And then, as you continue to walk in obedience with faith plus works, you can rest in the manifestation of God's will for your birth.

1 John 5:14-15 (ESV)
"And this is the confidence that we have toward him, that if we ask anything according to his will he hears us. And if we know that he hears us in whatever we ask, we know that we have the requests that we have asked of him."

It's amazing to rest in the confidence of a diligent prayer life! As long as your prayers are in God's will, you can trust that He hears you and that He will grant your request. What great power lies in our prayers to the Almighty God!

In fact, when you bathe your birth experience in prayer, God will often speak to you concerning your [33]perinatal season. At times, He will send you dreams to prepare you for your birth story and bring you peace about the outcome, or He will give you a vision that assures you your

---

[33] Perinatal: the period of time spanning pregnancy and the postpartum season

baby will be alright despite the particular circumstances that you will endure.

God sent a dream to one of my clients during her pregnancy, showing her that her baby would be healthy and would not need to be admitted to the Neonatal Intensive Care Unit (NICU). Before she reached 36 weeks of pregnancy, her water broke and we ended up at the hospital for preterm labor.

Instead of panicking or worrying, we praised and worshiped God during labor as I performed comfort techniques on my client's body and prayed. Her husband, too, was aligned with her faith for childbirth. And, when mama felt weak, he reminded her of her dream! This gave her strength to cross the finish line, and we welcomed a perfectly healthy baby girl into the world–without a NICU stay!

Prayer helps you and your baby to defy the odds and follow God's will for your bodies and your birth, rather than negative stereotypes or unfavorable statistics.

(3) Study to prepare for labor.

This is part of the "works" to add to your faith! Eliminate some of the fear of the unknown by learning. Take a comprehensive out-of-hospital childbirth education course to learn about physiological childbirth and your options within the medical system, as well as comfort techniques for labor, birth anatomy, and more. The class you select should be a minimum of four hours long in order to be thorough enough. ([34]Visit my website to learn about my online *Powerful Peace Birth Course*.)

---

[34] www.powerfulpeacedoula.com

Research. After taking a childbirth education class, you will better understand the realm of birth and discover what else you need to research. You will have a great foundation as well as tools to further your education in this area.

Hosea 4:6a (KJV) "My people are destroyed for lack of knowledge." Lack of knowledge equals ignorance. In the perinatal season, too many women die

> *Sister, be determined to destroy ignorance instead of letting ignorance destroy you.*

from preventable complications. Sister, be determined to destroy ignorance instead of letting ignorance destroy you.

(4) Strengthen your faith toward God and specifically for childbirth.

"So faith comes from hearing, and hearing through the word of Christ" Romans 10:17 (ESV).

Study scriptures to build your faith! The Bible is a holy book grounded in and crafted by faith; therefore meditating on the words of this book produces faith. (See Appendix F for scripture recommendations for childbirth.)

Pray for the faith you want! We serve a good Father who loves giving good gifts to His children (Matthew 7:9-11). And because faith is in God's will for His daughters, you can be confident that He will answer this prayer.

Sample prayer:

> *Lord, please increase my faith. You said that, with faith the size of a mustard seed, I can move mountains. I desire mountain-moving faith for childbirth! Please make my faith outshine any doubts and draw me closer to You and Your perfect will. Please sharpen my faith to believe You for Your best for me concerning pregnancy, labor, delivery, and my postpartum recovery. In Jesus' name, amen.*

As I mentioned within step one, expose yourself to stories of supernatural childbirth experiences from other like-minded moms. Whether through social media, books, podcasts, or face-to-face encounters, testimonies feed faith!

Also, when you are connected to a Christ-centered, prophetic church, you are likely to hear words that fuel your faith regularly. Repeat every faith-builder in your life! Whether scriptures, prayer, testimonies, sermons, or any form of God speaking to you personally, repetition facilitates learning. Be a faithful student, and God will make you a faith-filled disciple!

(5) Diminish voices of doubt/negativity in your life during pregnancy.

Galatians 5:7-9 (ESV)
"You were running well. Who hindered you from obeying the truth? This persuasion is not from him who calls you. A little leaven leavens the whole lump."

It only takes a little doubt to disrupt your faith in the birth room! Don't allow another person to tempt you towards fear and complaining during pregnancy or labor.

And don't discuss what you're asking God for with people who might respond with seeds of doubt or even with laughter. (See Joseph's story of sharing his dream with his brothers and father in Genesis chapter 37.) And if you unexpectedly receive a negative response, refrain from further discussion on the topic with that person.

In my first pregnancy, I shared my desires for supernatural childbirth with a friend, and she laughed in my face. I quickly understood that I needed to guard this birth dream in order to protect my faith. Do not assume that, just because your friend/associate is a Christian, he/she will understand or support your faith for childbirth.

Often, even followers of Christ compartmentalize their birth experiences and do not engage their faith in that area. Many view birth only as a physical experience rather than a spiritual one. Innocently, they might want to give you what they think are realistic expectations and warnings to prepare you for hardships like what they endured.

For some reason, moms tend to enjoy telling their birth experience as if it's the norm, like it's bound to happen to the next expectant mother. Recite scriptures in your mind while other moms tell you their horror stories of traumatic birth. Don't give the enemy room in your mind!

It's vital that your mind remain pure, focused on light. To read more vital keys to birth like you believe, continue to Part 2 of "How to Birth Like You Believe."

13

How to Birth Like You Believe, Part 2

Sister, let's review the first five points from Part 1:

1. Expose yourself to a new outlook on childbirth, discovering the possibilities.
2. Pray over your pregnancy, baby, body, labor, delivery, and postpartum recovery–daily!
3. Study to prepare for labor.
4. Strengthen your faith toward God and specifically for childbirth.
5. Diminish voices of doubt/negativity in your life during pregnancy.

And now we will resume with four more keys:

(6) Practice your "labor zone" 5-7 days per week, including your anchor points.

Sister, I am not preaching what I have not first practiced myself! During my first pregnancy, I dedicated 15-30 minutes of my daily prayer time to childbirth. My initial goal was to eliminate fear and breed confidence for birth, focusing on God. Since God designed childbirth, created my baby, and made me feel safe, I clung to Him in birth. In His presence, all of my anxieties melted away! I wanted them to STAY gone, so I continued …

I prayed over my pregnancy, labor, delivery, and post-partum recovery. I visualized myself in labor feeling peaceful, confident, and excited. By faith, I envisioned a birth story full of answered prayers, and I imagined what it would feel like to hold my baby in perfect health and gratitude.

I also prepared notecards with written scriptures and confessions that strengthened my faith. Over the course of the pregnancy, my stack of notecards grew weekly, and so did my peace. Mission accomplished! I approached my first labor with so much confidence that the medical professionals around me were astonished that I was that calm as a first-time mom. This was answered prayer on display!

I also noticed that I had practiced this zone so much that it became the natural flow of my labor zone: meditating on relevant scriptures, breathing deeply, trusting God for birth, exercising quiet calm, and worshiping God! I had memorized many of the scriptures and confessions that I had rehearsed, and during contractions, when I needed help the most, those powerful words resounded in my soul.

Because this worked so well for me the first time, I repeated an enhanced version of this process during my second pregnancy! And now, I encourage you to take ten minutes minimum during your daily quiet time with God to devote to childbirth preparation for your soul.

Establish anchor points. Anchor points ground you by reminding you of your labor zone. You should repeat these elements during pregnancy and in labor, practicing relaxation in your labor zone.

For example, if you plan to use aromatherapy in labor, use the same essential oils in your practice time as you pray and breathe deeply. Your brain will memorize this association to peace and faith-filled focus, anchoring you back to that zone when you sniff the same essential oils in labor. (Be careful to avoid using essential oils like clary sage during pregnancy *before* labor, as it is known to stimulate contractions.) Take a look at the following list of anchor points to include as you practice your labor zone during pregnancy:

- Worship music
- Deep breathing
- Prayer
- Meditation on the Word of God
- [35]Written affirmations/confessions & scriptures (Repeat the same ones and meditate on them!)
- Aromatherapy (optional)

---

[35] See www.powerfulpeacedoula.com/products for Christ-centered affirmation cards and scripture cards for birth.

- Dim lighting
- Pelvic mobility exercises (optional)
- Stretching or a resting position with good posture (avoid reclining)

(7) Pray for wisdom as you build your birth team.

Wherever you go and whatever you do, people always have the power to change the atmosphere. Whether for better or worse, people influence your birth experience! Your birth team consists of medical staff, possibly a labor [36]doula, and family or friends. You have the power to choose who comprises your birth team, so seek God's wisdom to guide your decisions.

Don't just select the closest hospital to your house! Pray that God leads you to the right medical providers, whether at a particular hospital, birth center, or at home with a midwife.

Make sure that whomever you choose to support you in labor is aware of your faith for childbirth and is supportive of that–whether your baby's father, your mom, mother-in-law, sister, or best friend.

Consider weekly prayer sessions with at least one member of your birth team, covering your specific prayer requests for pregnancy, labor, delivery, and your postpartum period. With this person, you should feel comfortable to share even what may sound like crazy faith. If this individual exhibits skepticism, sarcasm, or laughter at your prayer requests, seek to teach him/her.

---

[36] See Appendix H, "Definitions."

Do your best to educate your support team, even asking them to read *Birth Like You Believe* with you and take the [37]*Powerful Peace Birth Course* with you.

Plan this support team during pregnancy, beginning as early as you can so you have more time to prepare together. If your baby's father does not understand supernatural childbirth, add to your birth team another woman that you trust, whether a faith-filled mom, friend, or doula.

If anyone on your team instills doubt, fear, or opposing childbirth philosophies after thorough birth education, consider replacing that person with someone else who can better support you.

Also, hire a Holy Spirit-filled labor doula. Although it is not easy to find a Holy-Spirit-filled doula or what I like to call a "Kingdom doula," it is well worth the search and the investment if you can find one. Having a Kingdom doula at your birth adds another layer to the faith in the room! God can use her/him to progress labor in the specific ways your body needs when this birth professional is submitted to God and sensitive to His voice.

As your doula lays hands on you during comfort techniques for labor, the Spirit of God can work through her/his hands with the "laying on of hands" (as mentioned in Scripture) for supernatural progress in your body *and* peace in your soul.

There's power in having your doula to be an additional faith partner, adding expertise for natural progress to connection to God for spiritual progress. God can lead your doula with wisdom for your specific birth (for the

---

[37] See www.powerfulpeacedoula.com to order *Powerful Peace Birth Course.*

best position changes, comfort techniques, etc.), as all childbirth experiences are different. The wisdom that comes from God is quite a powerful enhancement to professional knowledge!

Interview doulas in advance and ensure your foundational doctrinal beliefs align and your personalities are compatible. Confirm that your doula is comfortable and confident praying over you aloud prenatally and during labor. (Note: Be cautious of allowing anyone to pray over you or your baby if you feel skeptical about the spiritual condition of this individual.)

If you cannot afford a labor doula and your insurance does not cover this expense, consider creating a "doula fund" that friends and family can contribute to at your baby shower and gender reveal party, if applicable. Another consideration is waiting to decorate your nursery and instead investing that money into your once-in-a-lifetime childbirth experience!

Babies are not picky about what their room looks like, and many babies don't even sleep in their cribs for the first several months of their lives anyway. They're instead [38]sleeping in their parents' room in a bedside bassinet, in a portable playpen with infant inserts, or in the bed with parents who choose to co-sleep. So why not invest more money up-front into higher chances of a smooth, peaceful, time-efficient labor–decreasing chances of maternal mortality/morbidity and birth trauma?

With maternal mortality rates as high as they are, I believe it's time to re-evaluate pregnancy priorities and make decisions with more long-lasting benefits: investing

---

[38] See www.brawleybabysleep.com for expert sleep training to help your baby sleep through the night consistently, improving brain development and mood and boosting their immune system.

in a thorough childbirth education course and hiring a labor doula.

If you still cannot afford hiring a doula after you've made financial sacrifices, prepare a close friend or family member to be as close to a doula for you as possible. Ask him/her to participate in a comprehensive childbirth education class with you and regularly practice the comfort techniques that he/she learns. And, Mama, you do the work to research well and prepare an action plan for each stage of labor. (Consider hiring a birth coach to help you prepare your plans.)

Your plans should include more detailed instructions than a traditional birth plan. This will help your designated birth companion to execute your wishes to the best of his/her ability. Be sure to include position changes, food, hydration, ambience for the room, and comfort techniques you want to try for different stages of labor.

During pregnancy, ask yourself these questions:

1. "After prayerful consideration, do I feel peaceful and confident about those on my birth team?" "Have I invited a friend or family member only to avoid hurting her/his feelings?" "What is the purpose of each member of my birth team? Are each of them able to properly fulfill these roles?"
2. "If money were not a hindrance, would I change the medical professionals on my team?" "Would I instead give birth at a birth center? Or at home with a midwife?" "Would I add my ideal doula to my team?"
3. "How have I engaged my faith in this process?" "Have I settled for something less than what I

believe God wants for me?" "Have I allowed doubt, fear, or negativity to influence any of my choices in this area?"

(8) Pack your anchor points in your birth bag.

Remember, your anchor points remind you of your labor zone. These elements provide positive associations that signal your brain to return to the state of relaxation and surrender that you practiced during pregnancy.

After rehearsing your labor zone during pregnancy, don't forget to pack your anchor points in your birth bag! In fact, ensure that your selected items are included on your [39]birth bag checklist.

Examples of anchor points:

- Notecards/posters/sticky notes:
    - Affirmations ([40]See my affirmation cards.)
    - Confessions
    - Scriptures (See my scripture cards for birth.)
- [41]Essential oils and diffuser

---

[39] Visit www.powerfulpeacedoula.com/products to download my free birth bag checklist.

[40] Visit www.powerfulpeacedoula.com/products to download my birth affirmation cards and scripture cards.

[41] You can purchase my recommendations for these products via my Amazon store through www.powerfulpeacedoula.com/products or on my Instagram or Facebook accounts, both labeled "Kirstie.Doula".

- Music playlists
- Bible (for those who prefer physical Bible)
- Visual object that brings you comfort (i.e. photo of pet or other child, baby onesie, sonogram)

(9) Set the atmosphere.

My favorite part about my home birth was the atmosphere! For this birth, I hung string lights from the ceiling, mounted posters on the walls (composed of scriptures and confessions), and dimmed the lighting. I played soft worship music, enjoyed an aromatherapy diffuser with warm, changing colors, and set my birth pool in front of the fireplace in my basement that I had saturated with prayer for nine months.

Oh, the peace and joy I experienced in this prepared place! Now, home is not your only option to create a meaningful atmosphere for birth. You can prepare the room anywhere you go!

Examples:

- Lighting
  - Dim lighting
  - Battery-operated candles
  - String lights
- Praise & worship music/uplifting instrumental music
- Aromatherapy
- Anointing oil on the doorposts, windows, bedpost or birth tub (not enough to drip, make a mess, or attract attention, haha!)

- Posters
  - Affirmations
  - Scriptures
  - Confessions
- Pray over the room as soon as you arrive at your birth location!
- Ask your support partner(s) to guard the peace of the room by taking some conversations to the hallway and reminding medical staff to use quiet voices and limit interruptions.

Sister, take these steps for how to birth like you believe and study them. I have lived these steps, and by God's grace and wisdom, I know the power that lies herein. I pray that God empowers you to apply self-discipline to employ all the knowledge you gain for childbirth. Couple this knowledge with your faith and tie it together with a trusted birth companion to help you.

14

Formula for Success

$\mathcal{W}$e are not omniscient beings, but there are some things we know for sure as it relates to birthing God's way. Use the "F.A.C.S." acronym as a summary to help you easily remember the formula for how to birth like you believe:

F.A.C.S.:

1. **F**aith
2. **A**ction
3. **C**ommunion with God
4. **S**upport

Faith

Notice what God's Word says about faith in the following passages of Scripture:

Matthew 17:20 (ESV)

"... For truly, I say to you, if you have faith like a grain of mustard seed, you will say to this mountain, 'Move from here to there,' and it will move, and nothing will be impossible for you."

Mark 11:22-24 (ESV)

"And Jesus answered them, 'Have faith in God. Truly, I say to you, whoever says to this mountain, 'Be taken up and thrown into the sea,' and does not doubt in his heart, but believes that what he says will come to pass, it will be done for him. Therefore I tell you, whatever you ask in prayer, believe that you have received it, and it will be yours.'"

Faith can move mountains! Pray, believe, and receive it. If you lack faith, expecting that your concerns are too big for God to handle, you will see few miracles. Pray and believe like you KNOW how big your God is. He is mightier than any mountain and more powerful than any problem! He is the Almighty, and even the winds and waves obey Him (See Matthew 8:27).

> *He is mightier than any mountain and more powerful than any problem!*

Faith is very important to God. God needs to be believed. In fact, faith is so important that God's Word says it's impossible to please Him without it! How can we birth like we believe if we do *not* believe? It's impossible to birth God's way without faith.

Hebrews 11:6 (KJV)
"But without faith it is impossible to please him: for he
that cometh to God must believe that he is, and that he is
a rewarder of them that diligently seek him."

One of faith's rewards is that you receive more from God. When you act like you know that your Heavenly Father is all-powerful, you ask for more. When you ask for more than the average mom for childbirth, you receive more.

Psalm 2:8 (ESV) says, "Ask of me, and I will make the nations your heritage, and the ends of the earth your possession." We see here that the Word specifies, "Ask." Some blessings are only off-limits to believers because they fail to ask. And it takes faith to ask for certain things that feel too big!

> *Some blessings are only off-limits to believers because they fail to ask.*

Although God's power is literally limitless, a lack of faith will limit God's power in *your* life. With big faith, you will receive more of the heritage that belongs to you as a daughter of God Almighty. And the heritage that I'm referring to in the context of birth is motherhood and childbirth according to God's original design—health, peace, wholeness, and joy!

Action

James 2:26 (NKJV)
"For as the body without the spirit is dead, so faith
without works is dead also."

Remember that we are not just spirit beings, but we do possess a body. It is important to take care of your body, knowing it is the temple of the Holy Spirit (1 Corinthians 6:19-20). You reap rewards in childbirth for taking care of your body and mind with good nutrition, exercise, stretching, chiropractic care, proper posture, doctor's appointments, and childbirth education.

Now, I must comment on fitness and nutrition:

I know that pregnancy fatigue and night wakings can make exercise feel like an unrealistic goal. But trust me, if you push yourself to exercise consistently, you will experience fewer pregnancy symptoms, you will have more energy, and your body will have greater stamina for labor.

Aim for 5 days per week, 3 days minimum; and seek assistance if you need help creating a suitable exercise routine for pregnancy. You may have a friend or family member who is knowledgeable in fitness and willing to help, or you can hire a personal trainer for pregnancy workouts. There are also multiple apps you can download to your phone that specialize in pregnancy workouts (You can search YouTube for videos as well).

Another challenge in pregnancy is maintaining a healthy diet. I am well aware that food aversions and various cravings tend to plague pregnancy. You can blame hormonal changes for those symptoms! However, do your best to eat plenty of protein (e.g. wild-caught salmon, antibiotic-free chicken, grass-fed beef), complex carbohydrates (e.g. sweet potatoes, brown rice), vegetables, fruit, and healthy fats (e.g. avocado, eggs, extra virgin olive oil).

If you experience aversions to vegetables, try switching to different kinds of vegetables than you normally eat. Or try consuming them in different forms: Blend them into a smoothie with fruit, or make a tasty salad with all your favorite toppings.

If you experience aversions to meat, try adding different sauces to mask the animal taste. You can also try eating your meat in pastas or soups.

With great nutrition, you'll notice your cravings decrease and your energy increase (among a host of other benefits!).

Another action to prepare for the best experience is hiring the right professionals for your birth team. Hire a labor doula and be careful to select your medical team and birth location with wisdom. Find out what their birth philosophy is and how it aligns with your goals. Ask questions like, "What's your c-section rate?" and "What's your rate of induction of labor?" If you are hoping for a natural birth, high rates of medicalized birth are red flags to avoid. (You will find a comprehensive list of questions for your healthcare provider, along with thorough explanation, in my [42]*Powerful Peace Birth Course.*) Ideally, you should begin the process of researching and conducting interviews in your first trimester.

Read about pregnancy, labor, and the postpartum period. Study the process, invest in useful [43]items, and research whatever you don't understand. Sister, do your best and trust God to do the rest!

Communion with God

Psalm 91:1-2 (KJV)
"He that dwelleth in the secret place of the Most High

---

[42] Visit www.powerfulpeacedoula.com.
[43] See my Amazon store for pregnancy, labor, and postpartum items: www.powerfulpeacedoula.com/products

shall abide under the shadow of the Almighty. I will say
of the Lord, He is my rock and my fortress: my God; in
Him will I trust."

Communion with God is intimate fellowship with Him
via worship, prayer, praise, Scripture and listening to God.
It provides safety, comfort, and peace in childbirth, no
matter the circumstance. By God's wisdom, you can make
the best decisions for you and your baby, even if it con-
flicts with medical determinations.

You know that you and your baby are safe when you're
in God's hands and you're
following His lead. He is the
only all-knowing One in the
room who makes no mistakes
and is not subject to human
error.

*He is the only all-
knowing One in the
room who makes no
mistakes and is not
subject to human
error.*

Intimate communion with
God during pregnancy, la-
bor, and the postpartum
period yields greater joy, better regulated blood pressure,
less tension, and ultimately greater birth satisfaction.
Communion with God also decreases depression and anxiety during pregnancy and the postpartum season. Who
would refuse these benefits?! God is infinitely good, and
intimate time with Him breeds multi-layered rewards
beyond our comprehension.

Support

Ecclesiastes 4:9-12 (ESV)
"Two are better than one, because they have a good
reward for their toil. For if they fall, one will lift up his

fellow. But woe to him who is alone when he falls and
has not another to lift him up! Again, if two lie together,
they keep warm, but how can one keep warm alone?
And though a man might prevail against one who is
alone, two will withstand him—a threefold cord is not
quickly broken."

When you add a faith-filled, childbirth-educated partner to your birth experience plus the Holy Spirit, you have
a threefold cord that is not easily broken. You, Sister, are
the third strand in that cord. And as you hang on to this
cord, you are less likely to be broken by complications,
delays, or discouragement in labor.

Refer to my [44]birth story when my mother objected to
the alternate course of action. Her faith sharpened my faith
when the cloudiness of "labor land" plus fatigue tempted
me to accept my doctor's ultimatum. She knew what I
truly desired and for what I had been praying.

With the prayers and tangible support of my husband
and mother plus all of the prayerful support of my family
members from afar, I was able to overcome the odds of
that situation when I most likely would have been unable
to do so alone.

Apply F.A.C.S. to your childbirth, whether you're
facing complications or not! Use this acronym as a formula
to birth like you believe.

When you birth like you believe, you will approach
childbirth with courage, peace, and authority of the Holy
Spirit within you. Mountains will look like mole hills in
the presence of your faith.

[44] See "My Birth Stories" in Appendix A.

15

———

Are You a Believer?

*I*f you have read *Birth Like You Believe* and want to be *sure* that you are a believer in Jesus Christ, pray the following prayer aloud from your heart:

> *Heavenly Father, in the name of Jesus, I confess that I am a sinner in need of Your grace. Please forgive me for my wrongdoing and wash me from the inside out.*
>
> *I confess with my mouth and believe in my heart that Jesus Christ is Lord. I confess that Jesus died on the cross for my sins, rose on the third day, and gained victory over death itself.*

I renounce unforgiveness and all other sins I have committed knowingly and ignorantly. I renounce all covenants I have made with any spirits or groups that are not of You. I plead the blood of Jesus to break any curses in my life. And please deliver me from all ungodly soul-ties with other people.

Lord, please fill me with Your Holy Spirit and heal all wounds of my soul. Fill me with Your desires. Stir within me great spiritual hunger for Scripture, prayer, and consistent involvement in Your church.

Thank You that Your strength is made perfect in my weakness, and Your grace is sufficient for me. Give me the grace and strength to seek You with my whole heart every day and never give up on You.

Thank You for Your love, mercy, and for the free gift of salvation. And please teach me how to love You the way You deserve. Lead me to birth like I believe, both biologically and spiritually! In Jesus' name, amen.

If you accepted Jesus in your heart for the first time or have just returned to Him, CONGRATULATIONS, my sister! Welcome to the family of God! I am so happy for you and all of Heaven is rejoicing, too! Woohoo!

You've just made the BEST decision of your life. And what better way to become a better mother than to start with salvation, healing, and deliverance for your SOUL?! May you pass down generational blessings to your baby and an inheritance of Perfect Love that is Jesus.

Appendix A
My Birth Stories:
Hospital & Home Birth

Childbirth #1: My Hospital Birth

I had prayed for a pain-free, short birth; but God answered those prayers with a "no." Although I believed with all my heart that I would experience a pain-free, quick birth, I learned later that it was not part of His will. However, I did experience supernatural childbirth, clearly touched by the hand of God with miracles, light, and strength. Let's dive in …

My first baby was born in a hospital on a military base in Landstuhl, Germany, in 2019. I was not a doula at this time, but I had done quite a lot of research. In retrospect, I still had important gaps in my knowledge base, and I failed to do several things that could have improved my experience.

I was not perfect in my knowledge, but I served a perfect God! He taught me much during that journey that I would not exchange for an easier adventure, even if I could. He opened my eyes to new revelations about childbirth, myself, faith, life, sacrifice, and how it all intersects.

Yes, God does bless some women with labor contractions that do not hurt; but that's not what God willed for me. I learned later that He wanted to teach me some things that I would not have learned if I had a short, easy birth. Life is not always "easy" and things don't always happen for us in the timeframe we prefer; but God is always good, sovereign, and strategic.

Although this labor was much longer and more painful than I had hoped, my testimony is that my soul did not suffer even while my body was in labor for nearly 40 hours. And, in addition to a perfectly healthy baby and mommy, my birth plan was executed in full. This was hard, long, and exhausting, but oh so worth it!

Keep in mind that I'm counting the start of labor from when contractions developed a pattern of being 10 minutes apart, preventing me from a good night's sleep! I did not sleep for two nights straight because contractions were 7-10 minutes apart the first night of early labor and then 3-5 minutes apart the second night of labor. I experienced intense contractions for around 30 hours.

I went to the hospital too soon and was sent back home, just to return again after several more hours.

Through it all, I never experienced even a little bit of fear, and all of my primary goals for my birth were met: No fear, no trauma, no pain medication, no despair, no vacuum or forceps, no c-section, no episiotomy, no Pitocin, no perineal tears, and no artificial rupture of membranes (breaking my water).

After I had been laboring at the hospital for more than 12 hours, my obstetrician told me that I had been laboring there for too long and that hospital protocol mandates intervention because of the lack of dilation progress. I had been around 5 or 6 centimeters dilated for several hours, meaning labor had stalled.

She insisted that, even though my baby was doing fine and so was I, protocol mandated she either break my water or give me Pitocin. She, then, harshly stated, "I can either break your water, give you Pitocin, or you *can* go home." By that point, my contractions were so strong, long, and frequent that it seemed like sarcasm for her to suggest an ultimatum like "agree to one of these medical interventions or go home."

My husband and mother were offended by her tone and ultimatum, and one of them asked the nurse to talk to the doctor about her attitude.

I assumed the obstetrician was blunt with me because she had read my very detailed birth plan and knew that I wanted to labor spontaneously, without medical intervention (unless necessary for the health and safety of me or my baby). Thus, she forcefully presented these undesirable options.

At the time, I was so consumed in my "labor zone" that I had very little emotion towards the ultimatum. I responded, "If I have to choose one, I guess you can break my water."

Since both my husband and my mother had read my birth plan, my mother spoke up and asked, "Kirstie, that's not really what you want, right?" And then she proceeded to delay the decision by distracting the doctor, saying she was going to call the obstetrician's superior.

Another part of this testimony is that my mother had met a man on the airport shuttle on her way to my house ... They had great conversations, and the man appreciated my mother's warm, friendly demeanor and substantive topics.

She also mentioned to him that she was on her way to

visit her pregnant daughter who lived in Germany. To her surprise, this man was a governing authority over multiple hospitals, including the one in which I was scheduled to deliver my baby!

He gave her his business card and urged her to contact him if she or I needed anything or if we wanted to share any feedback from my experience at one of the hospitals under his jurisdiction. Divine connection–you think?!

During the time my mother was calling her God-sent acquaintance, everyone left the room except for me and my husband. The doctor said she would return in about 30 minutes. Meanwhile, my husband and mother spoke to the nurse about the doctor's attitude, informing her that, unless the obstetrician could return with a better attitude, they would like to request a different doctor.

I was in the hydrotherapy tub praying silently and breathing deeply.

Inwardly I prayed, "Lord, I know You've heard my prayers throughout this pregnancy and labor; and I know that You can break my water and dilate my cervix to 10 centimeters. *And* I know You can do it quickly! Please Lord, do it now before the doctor returns!"

My husband then asked me, "Kirstie, I know what the doctor is saying and what your mother is saying, but what do YOU want to do? I responded, "I know God has heard my prayers, and I believe He can dilate me to 10 cm and break my water. And, He can do it quickly." Then he and I prayed aloud together.

When we finished, my mother returned to the room and asked me the same question: "Kirstie baby, what do you want to do?" And I answered her the same way I answered my husband. She then prayed over me aloud.

I started to wonder if my water had broken ... I noticed

tiny bubbles next to me in the tub, and I thought to myself, "How would I know when my water breaks if I'm in water?" So, I got out of the tub and onto the birth ball.

While on the birth ball, my mother read to me a text message containing a prayer from my sister Neiel. Immediately following that prayer, I stood to go to the bathroom and consequently noticed that my water had broken onto the birth ball!

The three of us rejoiced and praised God, and my labor contractions intensified! They felt like they were so long and frequent that they were overlapping, eliminating breaks in between. The sensations were so intense that, for the first time in labor, I struggled to breathe deeply. After breathing reminders from a kind nurse, I pushed myself to regain control over my breathing patterns.

Through it all, I never felt tempted to say words like, "I can't ..." nor to request pain medication at any point in labor, not even at this moment. In less than 30 minutes, God broke my water and dilated me to 9 centimeters!

The obstetrician returned with a much better attitude, and when she checked my cervix, she was amazed! She said, "Wow, well, if you can progress to 9 cm that fast on your own, I'll come back in 30 more minutes and see where you are then!"

In about 10-15 minutes from that point, I had the urge to push! The nurses insisted that I wait until I was checked again to ensure I was 10 cm dilated so that I did not swell my cervix by pushing while only 9 cm dilated. My instincts took over and it felt nearly impossible to stop pushing, so I told them I could not help but push and that they needed to call the doctor back into the room immediately.

When the doctor checked me, sure enough, I was already 10 cm dilated! A wave of joy, relief, excitement, adrenaline, and energy flooded my body! And after almost 40 hours of labor contractions, 2 nights of sleep deprivation, and very little food, I felt like the female hulk: stronger than ever!

I pushed for less than 20 minutes with the nurses, obstetrician, and my husband all cheering me on and affirming how great of a job I was doing.

And finally, I delivered my precious baby girl, 7 pounds 13.5 ounces, vaginally without pain medication and completely in the peace of God! After I pushed her out, I was on a "birth high," feeling like I was on top of a mountain. I felt more powerful than I had in my whole life!

The medical team praised me for how calm and controlled I was during labor, saying, "Are you sure you're a first-time mom?!" And a few days after delivery, one of my friends who was a hair stylist told me something interesting that her client (who was an obstetrician) said …

While getting her hair done, this obstetrician described a beautiful Black woman who gave birth a "few days ago" and birthed like a "rock star"! She described the calm and control that this first-time mom exuded, as well as how quickly her labor progressed during active labor (6-10 cm dilation) and how easily she pushed out her baby!

This same doctor who had been very rude to me told her hairstylist, "If I ever have a baby, I want to give birth exactly like she did!" My friend immediately told the doctor, "I know her! That's my friend, Kirstie!"

Although I did not experience a pain-free birth, I did experience a supernatural childbirth:

1. Supernatural acceleration after a long stall (See Isaiah 60:22)
2. Peace that surpasses all understanding (See Philippians 4:7)
3. God's strength made perfect in my weakness (See 2 Corinthians 12:9)
4. Fearlessness in the perfect love of God (See 1 John 4:18)

I appreciated my baby even more after the travail for her birth; and, thankfully, through the long hours and severe pain, I never felt like this labor was more than I could bear (See 1 Corinthians 10:13).

Childbirth #2: My Water Birth at Home

My second childbirth experience was amazing! It was a planned water birth at my home in Alexandria, Virginia. Oh, the peace, joy, and safety I felt!

Before I took a pregnancy test, I was praying and the Holy Spirit told me, "You are pregnant. And this birth experience will be from glory to glory." He explained to me how the second one would be better than the first, and I immediately clung to that with faith in my heart.

My second birth experience was much shorter than the first, which fact alone made it better, haha! If counting labor from the onset of a regular contraction pattern, my labor was about 16 hours total. If counting labor by the medical definition of labor–active labor beginning at 6 cm dilation–, my labor was less than 4 hours long.

When early labor began, my husband and I were at the mall walking around and then eating at an Italian restaurant. Contractions were around seven to ten minutes apart at that time, and we peacefully enjoyed what I knew would be our last big meal before we met our precious baby Elias.

During our meal, contractions intensified to the point where I had to pause and breathe through them, but they were not painful. My husband got a little concerned and wanted to rush back home, but I assured him that I would not deliver the baby in the restaurant, haha! We had enough time to finish our meal in peace and excitement.

After eating, we returned home and I called my midwife to inform her of early labor. She instructed me to get in bed and rest as long as I could. With my worship music playing and aromatherapy diffuser going, I dozed in and out of sleep in bed from 8:00 p.m. to about 5 a.m., minus trips to the bathroom and kitchen. Once I presumed active labor had begun, I headed to my basement, which I had prepared as my birth space.

As soon as I got into the basement, I began to cry tears of joy and excitement.

I had scriptures, affirmations, and confessions posted on the walls. I had hung ambient string lights and had my aromatherapy diffuser turned on with warm, colored lighting and soothing fragrances. My birth pool was in the center of the room in front of the fireplace, and my bluetooth speaker was already in place to play my music aloud.

Since I had already been praying in this space 3-5 days a week and practicing my labor zone here, I felt a powerful sense of fulfillment. My labor zone was a worship zone! And it felt like I had entered into the sanctuary of the house of God. I felt safe and whole in His arms.

I was thrilled to labor for my son, and I could feel the prayers I had prayed over that space so many days during pregnancy in preparation for this very moment. God answered, and I was in a glorious worship experience. No fear: just faith, peace, and excitement!

The Holy Spirit was clearly there, and I was overjoyed to be in the privacy of my home where I could pray out-loud, speak in [45]tongues, cry, and even laugh in the Holy Spirit as I was filled with unspeakable joy.

As I prayed and worshiped God, I also moved my pelvis in various ways to make more room for my baby to get into ideal positioning for delivery. My husband and mom were still busy working to fill up the birth pool with warm water, so my husband helped me with comfort techniques sparingly until they finished.

They got the pool filled just in time, and I was able to utilize it for additional relief! When my birth assistant arrived about three hours before delivery, she remained fairly quiet saying that I had everything under control and was doing very well. My midwife arrived two hours or less before delivery, and she said something like, "Well, you're doing perfectly on your own so keep doing what you're doing!"

They pretty much stayed out of my way, and my husband and mom remained diligent with feeding me snacks, offering me water, managing my essential oils for different stages of labor, and following along with the "Labor To-Do List" I had created for them, haha.

---

[45] See Mark 16:17, Acts 2:4, and 1 Cor. 14:2.

(I did not have a doula because I did not find a local doula who aligned with my faith for childbirth along with a good personality connection! And for me, those were non-negotiable factors. Thus, I created a "Labor To-Do List" for my husband and mother to follow, which was like a super detailed birth plan with numerous non-medical wishes.)

During pregnancy, I prayed that I would labor during the night while my daughter was asleep and that she would be able to wake up in the morning and witness me pushing out her brother. I wanted her to know that I was not just babysitting someone else's newborn, but that he was the one who had been occupying mommy's tummy and was here to stay!

As another answered prayer, she was just waking up as I began the pushing stage! I asked my mother to bring Elaina downstairs, and she witnessed her brother's birth.

After less than four hours of what I perceived as active labor, he was born in the water. Although he was 9 pounds 1.5 ounces with a head in the 99th percentile for newborns, I experienced no tearing! This was another answered prayer.

After I met my son, the midwife kept telling me to talk to my baby because I was still in my labor zone–which was a worship zone!–simply repeating "Thank You, Jesus" in between kissing Elias. My heart was overflowing with gratitude.

I was especially excited about the timing of this birth since my midwives had wanted to begin natural induction methods that Wednesday at 11:00 a.m. if I were still pregnant. But, my son was born by 9:00 a.m. that same day! (I was 8 days past my estimated due date, the same timeframe as my first delivery.)

After both births, I experienced a beautiful birth high, never to feel the baby blues, postpartum depression, nor any kind of postpartum mood or anxiety disorder. I am thankful for God's peace, joy, and grace for the journeys!

Appendix B
My Family's Birth Stories

The power of God has been evident in birth stories of women in my own family! In fact, the birth story of my older sister, Neiel, inspired me to ask God for a supernatural childbirth of my own. She was the first person who exposed me to what childbirth could look like when women break the curse and birth like God originally intended. About eight years before I birthed my first child, my personal journey of detaching fear from childbirth began after hearing Neiel's story of supernatural childbirth. I hope that, as you read the birth stories of some of the women in my family, you will feel inspired to birth like you believe.

Neiel's Supernatural Childbirth

I remember being in labor with my first baby early on March 3rd, 2012, but I didn't know it. Cramps in my lower abdomen disturbed my sleep throughout the night. I was in and out of the bathroom. I figured that this was another episode of Braxton Hicks contractions. I remember turning on my phone researching and researching the difference between the fake contractions and the real ones. I could be in labor, I thought. No, maybe I'm not.

Hours later, the sun lit my bedroom more and more. Before I knew it, my whole room was full of sunlight and the cramps hadn't stopped. I told my husband that I might be in labor. He told me to take a shower just in case, so I did. As I began dressing for the hospital, my water broke. It was time. I knew it. My husband and I got fully ready and left for the hospital.

When I arrived at the hospital, the doctor checked me. I was 4 cm dilated. I wasn't going back home until I had my baby. I remember being in the birthing room. The lights were dim. All was quiet. But, my mind wasn't silent. It was as though Heaven's radio played in my head. I heard songs I knew and ones I didn't know. At one moment, my husband placed headphones in my ears with worship music playing. It didn't help. Immediately, I took them out of my ears and again, Heaven's radio played.

Along the way, I reached about 6 cm and the doctor told me if I didn't continue progressing, she would give me Pitocin. I didn't want Pitocin because of the horror stories my mom told me. So, I prayed. My husband prayed. My mom prayed. Within one hour, I began progressing again. I didn't need Pitocin, and I was grateful.

After nearly 12 hours of labor, my contractions never felt stronger than my worst menstrual cramp. It never became unbearable. The peace of God saturated my birthing room. It was a peace I couldn't comprehend.

Once I was ready to push, the nurse was amazed

because she told me that it didn't seem like it was my first birth, though it was. I pushed for about 10 minutes or less. My sweet baby girl arrived safely without any complications. And as I was being wheeled to the recovery room, I told myself, "I can't wait to do this again!"

–Neiel (Bronner) Zimbron

My Mother's 5th Birth

My mother had four babies vaginally, including a set of identical twins (that's me and my twin!). Before her fifth delivery, God sent my mother a prophetic word: "You will go through in peace and there will be a quick release."

She testified saying, "The moment that I heard those words, I knew that it was concerning the delivery of my fifth child. Consequently, I had perfect peace when I was told that I had to have a scheduled c-section because I instantly remembered the prophetic word that was spoken over me."

My mother confidently approached her planned c-section delivery and experienced perfect peace during and after the surgery!

She did not realize until later that she had experienced a supernatural childbirth. Her surgery proceeded without complications. Her baby and her body maintained perfect health! She encountered zero adverse effects of the medication used for surgery. And her recovery was "easy," she said! It did not aggravate her c-section incision to cough, laugh, climb stairs, or transition into or out of bed. Of all the complaints women have after c-sections, my mother could not relate to any of them! She said that was her easiest, quickest, most peaceful birth of all!

Babies born via c-section delivery are at a higher risk of

degraded gut health in comparison to babies born vaginally. They are also at a higher risk of developing asthma and food and environmental allergies. Despite the odds, my brother has not experienced any of these conditions as a result of being born via c-section!

Truly, the safest place to be is in the will of God, no matter where that is.

My Twin's Birth Center Childbirth

At first, as many young women do, I feared labor and childbirth. Then, I read testimonies of women who believed God for peace and miracles throughout pregnancy, labor, and delivery, and who experienced minimal pain and maximum peace! My faith was built, and I became excited about what God would do! I wrote a list of requests and confessions before God, and I took it to Him in prayer frequently.

My pregnancies with both my daughter and my son were supernatural! God answered my prayers for no complications, perfect health, and even energy to exercise during both of my pregnancies! I was working out until 40 weeks carrying BOTH of my babies!

When I arrived at the birth center while in labor with my firstborn, Isabella, the midwife told me that there was meconium in the fluid. Therefore, she might need to transfer me to a hospital because the baby's heart rate might drop. My husband and I prayed and asked for an alternative, so she allowed us to be monitored and to stay.

The baby's heart rate did not drop during the whole labor experience! My labor felt long, 21 hours, but God gave me peace, strength, and power through it. I asked God for a fully natural, unmedicated birth, and God gave me just that! I never even asked for medication, haha! It was manageable the entire time–as I prayed, worshiped God, recited scripture, and wore my husband's hands OUT with the counterpressure on my back during each contraction! (My husband was such a champ!)

I also asked God to help me stretch wide enough that I did not tear at all. God did it! My first baby was 8 lbs 7 oz. and my midwife was SHOCKED that I did not tear!

I asked God for no postpartum depression but for extreme joy, and I experienced an overwhelming joy when I held my daughter in my arms in that moment and during the weeks to come.

I had such an amazing experience giving birth to my daughter, and even such a beautiful recovery that the enemy started telling me that the next baby would be hard for me–that it couldn't possibly be this good again.

–Kristie (Bronner) Brawley

My Twin's Surprise Home Birth

Well, 2 years later, I had my son, and God OUTDID Himself! I asked God for the second birth to be a fraction of the time of the first one, and God went the extra mile! My water broke at 1:00 a.m., just like it did the first time while sleeping.

But this time, I waited in the bed, assuming it would be a while. I prayed, texted my doula and my mom, and went back to sleep. Around 4:00 a.m., I got up to shower and then I started timing my contractions. The app said "GO TO THE HOSPITAL NOW!" after timing only one contraction! I called my doula, my twin, and she firmly co-signed that instruction, haha!

I was laboring on my exercise ball in the bathroom at this

point, and I couldn't bring myself to get up because the contractions were coming so fast. But I was excited, at peace, and listening to my worship music.

My husband started tossing clothes at me telling me to hurry and get in the car. But I told him that the baby was about to come and that I absolutely could NOT get in the car! He didn't believe me until I showed him the baby's head crowning! I asked him to set the bath water, and this time he listened! Haha!

After about 10 minutes standing over the tub, our son was falling out and my husband was catching him! But I heard my husband telling our doula via phone that the baby was VERY blue, his umbilical cord was wrapped twice around his neck, and he wasn't breathing! My husband was calm but concerned and asked her what to do. He didn't know if our son was still alive or not.

I felt the peace of God, and I knew in my spirit that he was just fine. My husband unwrapped the cord, waited a couple seconds, and our son started crying. Our son was born around 6:00 a.m., only 2 hours after getting out of bed! I could not have asked for a better experience. No one else could make it to assist us, but GOD was with us every step of the way. He truly did exceedingly, abundantly, and above all we could ask or think!

Oh, and, again I requested not to tear. This baby was 9 lbs. 8 oz.–even larger than the first–and God helped me stay fully intact–NO tearing! And despite the fear that the enemy tried to bring about my emotional state postpartum, I experienced postpartum JOY again! And this postpartum season–with my beautiful toddler relaxing with me and my handsome baby boy–was even BETTER than the first go round! God truly answered my prayers that my birth experiences would be from glory to glory, better and better!

–Kristie (Bronner) Brawley

Appendix C
My Clients' Birth Stories, Part 1

The birth stories you will read here are the stories of some of my clients over time. And I don't consider these to be just ordinary stories, but testimonies of the goodness of God! Not every story appears ideal; but in every story, we witness the hand of God moving to do things that human beings could not do. To me, there are various kinds of stories that represent supernatural childbirth. Supernatural childbirth happens when God puts His "super" on our "natural" and gives us more than we could attain on our own.

I pray that these stories open your heart to the many possibilities of how God can show up during your birth.

Client #1

Oh, what an awesome time of worship we had during this labor experience! Although it was long and tiring on many levels, God was glorified and testimonies arose …

Client #1 was experiencing a very long labor that eventually led to her obstetrician suggesting a c-section. The obstetrician claimed that my client's pelvis was too narrow and that the baby was up too high. Because the baby was in an occiput posterior (OP) position (AKA sunny side up), the doctor stated that the narrow pelvic outlet would decrease the chances that this OP positioned baby would make it past the pelvic bone.

As soon as the doctor left the room, I prayed over Client #1 and her husband and encouraged them. And the power of God filled the room! All three of us began praising God aloud, worshiping God, and speaking scriptures one after the other, rotating organically who would speak next.

We had two hours before the next cervical exam when the doctor planned to further discuss performing a c-section if Client #1 had not progressed enough. By the time the nurse checked my client again, the baby had turned all the way around to an occiput anterior (OA) position, ideal for delivery! She was also 10 cm dilated and 100% [46]effaced, meaning the cervix was fully prepared for delivery.

The doctor was still skeptical about whether or not my client would be able to push the baby out past her pelvis, so she suggested some practice pushes. This obstetrician was shocked by how effectively Client #1 began pushing, even with an epidural! (Note: First-time moms with epidurals often push for 2-3 hours.)

Against the odds, God helped my client to push her baby out in around 30 minutes! She, herself, claimed that she did not know what she was doing. But, God did that!

---

[46] Effacement (noun): the thinning and shortening of the cervix during labor

Client #2

What Client #2 did not know is that I was fasting during the time of her delivery, a pre-planned fast that just so happened to overlap with the time of her birth. I was praying and fasting about a few different prayer requests during that time, but the timing turned out to be divine … God answered so many prayers and left us all in a whirlwind of awe and gratitude!

Now, let me give you a little background information on this case: Client #2 was very nervous and anxious about labor because she wrestled with anxiety even before pregnancy. During pregnancy, we prayed a lot, even scheduling video calls to pray, to breathe and to encourage her.

After remaining pregnant more than one week beyond her estimated due date, she wanted her labor to be medically induced. While at the hospital waiting for her body to respond to the induction drugs, she called me around 3:30 a.m.

Unfortunately, she explained to me how slow and frustrating the process was and how her baby's heart rate was decelerating too much. The medical team informed her that, if her baby's heart rate did not improve by morning, they would proceed with the drug Pitocin or proceed with a c-section delivery. With this news, she felt stressed and discouraged!

I prayed over her and suggested a specific position for her to try. In less than 30 minutes from that time, she informed me that her body had finally gone into labor and that her baby's heart rate was perfect!

Before labor, she told me that she did not want the drug Pitocin in her body, which is routinely administered during induction of labor. We prayed, asking God to help her body go into labor without the use of Pitocin. God clearly answered that with a "yes"!

She later told me that, when I prayed for her around 3:30 a.m., she felt "revival"! She said that word was the best way she could describe how she felt.

On my way to the hospital, I prayed and worshiped God the whole time, which is routine for me on my way to support clients in labor. This time, I had also called my mother and twin sister on the phone to agree with me in prayer.

We prayed that the baby would be born by 1:00 p.m., and the baby was born at 12:10 p.m.! We also prayed that she would have a very short pushing stage, less than 30 minutes. She pushed for less than 10 minutes before her baby was born!

The average length of active labor for a first-time mom is 12 hours; but Client #2 only experienced around 2 hours of what medical professionals in the U.S. consider to be active labor (between 6-10 cm dilation).

She birthed her baby without an epidural, which was her goal; and she had a labor experience that was started by God and accelerated by God! ... All the while, keeping her baby's heart rate in a healthy range, despite the dangerous heart decelerations the baby experienced before our 3:30 a.m. prayer time.

The peace of God was in the room, and it truly was a heavenly welcome for this precious baby girl.

Client #3

Client #3 had a 4.5-hour pushing stage and was completely exhausted after 20+ hours of unmedicated labor! When she decided that she wanted an instrument-assisted delivery, I fervently prayed that she nor her baby would experience any adverse effects of this vacuum-assisted delivery. I also prayed that her [47]perineum would not tear since the use of forceps and vacuum can significantly increase the risk of tearing.

I witnessed the obstetrician yank the vacuum with very aggressive technique, leaning backwards while pulling, adding her body weight in a manner that should not have been done! She did not seem confident in her ability to use the vacuum, as she attempted to dissuade my client from an instrument-assisted delivery.

The vacuum popped off the baby's head around four times as the doctor vigorously yanked the instrument. While witnessing these events and knowing that Client #3 was too tired to push in positions that would allow gravity to aid the process, I prayed even harder!

Thankfully, God chose to answer with a big fat "YES," and her perineum miraculously remained intact! More importantly, her baby suffered no injuries from the vacuum-assisted delivery, even with the poor technique that was used.

With the help of the Holy Spirit, along with her birth team, Client #3 was able to overcome the odds and experience a vaginal delivery without an epidural or opioid pain medication. She delivered a perfectly healthy baby and was able to achieve her primary birth goals.

Although this labor journey was long and tiring, it was

---

[47] Perineum (noun): the tissue connecting a woman's vagina and anus

filled with the peace and joy of the Holy Spirit. In fact, the majority of labor included jokes and laughter! My client's husband filled the atmosphere with humor and compliments; I filled the room with prayer, encouragement, and coaching; and Client #3 filled the room with the perseverance of a fighter–greater than what she thought possible.

Client #4

During pregnancy, God sent a meaningful dream to Client #4. In this dream, God showed her that she would deliver her baby early (specifying which month) and that the baby would not need treatment in the Neonatal Intensive Care Unit (NICU). God also showed her that she would not experience genital tears in childbirth!

Client #4 delivered her baby exactly one month before her estimated due date. During labor when she became discouraged by the intensity and length of labor, her husband read her affirmation note cards aloud. One of those cards recounted that powerful dream from the Lord. When he read this, we could feel strength from the Holy Spirit filling the room, and it was a mighty, moving moment!

She ended up having a vaginal delivery with a very short pushing stage, less than 30 minutes. Just like the dream had predicted, Client #4 experienced zero genital tearing, and her premature baby did not need to visit the NICU. Praise God!

Client #5

Client #5 was in labor about 36 hours total, and about 21 hours without an epidural. When she was examined and told she was only 6 centimeters dilated, she became very discouraged because she had already been in labor for around 34 hours by that point.

I told her the testimony of my first labor experience: how long it was and how, through prayer, God helped my cervix to dilate from 5 or 6 cm to 9 cm within 30 minutes, breaking my water within that timeframe also! And then, 10-15 minutes later, helped me to dilate to 10 cm. That was not because I knew all the right things to do back then, but truly through the power of prayer and faith!

After sharing my testimony with her, I prayed for her before her next cervical exam. And during this next cervical exam, which was less than 30 minutes after this prayer, the medical staff declared her cervix "complete," 100% effaced and 10 centimeters dilated!

This was about 2 hours since the previous cervical exam when she was 6 cm dilated. For a first-time mom, it would not be unusual for her cervix to take at least 1-2 hours to dilate one centimeter, which would mean that a normal pace would yield probably less than 8 cm dilated by that point.

Client #5, her husband, and I were all amazed at the power of God, faith, and the answered prayer!

I asked Client #5 to tell me how long she would like her pushing stage to be. I said, "Tell me _____ minutes or less that you'd like to push." She said, "Thirty minutes or less," so I prayed that God would help her to push the baby out in 30 minutes or less.

Because she was a first-time mom with an epidural, the average length of pushing would have been more like 2-3 hours. That's in the "natural." But, when God put His "super" on her "natural," she supernaturally pushed out her baby in 2-3 contractions after the doctor arrived, certainly less than 30 minutes!

Even though her labor was long, she was only in active labor for around 5 hours (active labor = 6+ centimeters dilation), which is less than half the average length of active labor for a first-time mom (12 hours).

The use of epidural anesthesia also increases the risk of genital trauma, but she had no perineal tears! She had a tear so small on her labia that the doctor could not even call it a first degree tear (which is the least severe form of genital tearing in childbirth). What an awesome God we serve!

Appendix D
My Clients' Birth Stories, Part 2

Client #6

Client #6 came to me with heavy emotional trauma from her first birth in which she experienced an unplanned c-section during the pushing stage because her doctor told her that her pelvis was too small for the size of her baby. She felt inadequate and began doubting her ability to vaginally birth babies.

She desperately desired to birth her second baby vaginally. After praying, presenting reassuring facts, and encouraging her, she and I, along with her husband, were ready to attempt a vaginal birth after cesarean (VBAC).

This attempt was truly "against the odds" since her doctor had done his calculations and had come to the conclusion that she was not a good candidate for a VBAC. He was unwilling to so-called "take that risk" with her.

Triumphantly, she pushed her baby out while that doctor walked into the labor and delivery room!

Client #7

Client #7 birthed her baby two months before her estimated due date, and God showed up to make this a sweet, peaceful birth anyway ...

She and I had both prayed that I would be able to be there, and God answered that with a "yes," even with sporadic timing. It was a Friday, and I had just returned from a vacation in Italy with my husband. I was scheduled to leave for a work trip the following Monday morning. This baby was born on Saturday morning in perfect timing for me to support this precious family, even with a premature delivery!

What she did not know was that, on my flight home from Italy, I was fasting and praying about a few things, which included her baby's health and her labor and delivery. I had prayed for miracles in the birth room! As soon as I landed in Atlanta and turned on my phone, I received a text message about her medically necessary induction of labor that was to begin that day.

As a first-time mom, the medical team expected that it would take around three days to induce her labor; but instead, contractions began later that same night! (This was without the use of synthetic oxytocin [Pitocin], only with artificial prostaglandins. And that's quite rare!)

The next morning, labor had intensified, and I prayed my whole way to the hospital, calling my twin and my mother to agree with me in prayer. I prayed that, when I walked into the room, God would supernaturally accelerate labor.

When I walked in, my client's demeanor was not that of a mom in active labor, and her contractions were still about 5 minutes apart. Maybe 30-45 minutes after my arrival, her contractions had progressed to 2-3 minutes apart, and she was clearly in active labor. God had answered!

I had also prayed that Client #7 would deliver by noon. She delivered at 11:38 a.m.! I prayed that she would push for less than 30 minutes before the baby was born, and she pushed for 20 minutes or less! She had no perineal tears and needed no genital stitching.

She had originally desired a home birth, which is not allowed for premature deliveries. I had prayed over the medical team that would support her in the hospital, and God blessed her with a hospital midwife who operated more like a home birth midwife than any of the hospital midwives I've seen!

She took a hands-off approach and allowed Client #7 to push out her baby and her placenta spontaneously and peacefully, rather than rushing the process.

In total, her labor was less than 24 hours, which is very short for a first-time mom who experienced medical induction of labor. Her active labor was around 2 hours long, in contrast to the average of 12 hours for first-time moms. And most importantly, she and her baby completed labor in great health and safety. Praise God!

Client #8

Client #8's demeanor throughout labor did not appear as if she were in active labor at all! When I met her and her husband at the hospital, I looked at her and immediately thought that she would be sent back home for arriving too early.

Although the spacing of her contractions at home clearly warranted hospital admission, her mannerisms and facial expressions did not convince me that her contractions had the strength to push out a baby just yet. I did not say anything but encouraging words out-loud, of course.

Even the nurse who prepared to check Client #8's cervix tried to prepare her before the exam for the possibility of being sent back home because she did not appear to be experiencing intense contractions! Looking at the contraction monitor, her contractions still did not appear to be intense.

To our surprise, she was already 5 or 6 cm dilated upon arrival at the hospital. She opted for an epidural for her first birth and was hoping for an unmedicated birth this time around, with the help of her doula of course (She did not have a doula during her first birth.). God answered "yes" to helping her achieve an unmedicated birth this time around!

After being admitted to a labor and delivery room, we prayed, turned up her instrumental playlist, and her husband even served communion! Because I am an ordained minister, he asked me to facilitate communion, and it was a beautiful experience. Oh, what peace of God was in that birth room!

Her husband also pulled some anointing oil out of their hospital bag and anointed the hospital bed. The presence of God was clearly there, and we worshiped the Lord as Client #8 labored and as I performed comfort techniques for her body.

Among many prayers, we prayed that she would experience a short pushing stage, and she did! She pushed for 15 minutes, even though I did not consider the baby to be low enough to warrant a 15-minute pushing stage. I wanted her to wait longer and labor the baby down lower to ensure a shorter pushing stage, but she became impatient and wanted to begin pushing as soon as the doctor confirmed that she was 10 cm dilated. Whatever the client wants, she gets!

So, we covered the experience in prayer, and God answered! Her husband had been praying during the pregnancy that his son would be born on his daughter's birthday. And although that date was a few weeks before his wife's estimated due date, God answered that, too!

What rejoicing when this baby was born on his sister's birthday! He emerged after prayer, communion, anointing oil, worship, praise, and only a 15-minute pushing stage ... and after less than 6 hours of active labor that did not appear to be intense enough to cross the finish line. What a blessing!

Client #9

Client #9 had many reasons to walk away from her birth experience feeling traumatized ... reasons beyond any of our control. To the human eye, she did everything right! She did her research, took my 6-hour comprehensive childbirth education class, hired a professional labor doula (me), and solicited emotional and spiritual support from her baby's father and her mother during labor.

She had a great birth team! Together, we prayed, performed comfort techniques on Client #9's body, put her in optimal positions for labor progression, and encouraged her. She labored at a birth center with excellent midwives and nurses surrounding her as well.

She engaged phone calls from her father and other relatives and church members interceding on her behalf and praying powerful prayers over her. I, her baby's father, and her mother prayed over her aloud. She danced during labor, did her best to smile, and most importantly, worshiped the Lord!

Client #9 had worship music playing throughout labor, and we enjoyed an atmosphere of worship, even when circumstances were discouraging. With every unfavorable report from the medical team, we prayed and worshiped God even more, extending our faith! The presence of the Lord was so evident in the birth space that the staff could feel it. A nurse walked in and exclaimed, "Wow, I feel the presence of God in here!"

Still, my client's baby would not descend far enough to promote the cervical dilation we needed. The baby's head was in an awkward position for descent, and mom's contractions persisted in an irregular pattern on and off. We tried positions that utilized gravity, various stretches to release key ligaments, positions to change the baby's position, the breast pump, and much more. Still, her contractions were insufficient and inconsistent.

After over 48 hours of intense contractions and maybe around 20 hours at the birth center, the midwife on duty decided it was time for a hospital transfer. As compassionately as she could, she stated, "I've seen you guys try all the things ... You've done everything right, and there's nothing left to try. With all that I've seen you guys doing in here, we should have had a baby by now. Your labor has been stalled for several hours, and there's gotta be a reason. Unfortunately, it's time to transfer you to the hospital."

My client melted in tears. Her mom and baby's father were exhausted and discouraged. Once the medical staff exited the room, I again prayed over the family.

The hospital transfer was rough to say the least. Several

hours passed before my client was able to be admitted to a room. Since she had been laboring for over 55 hours, she wanted an epidural to escape the longevity of the pain. But unfortunately, she had to wait hours before receiving that epidural! Among several issues she encountered at this hospital, my client later described her experience there as "awful."

The doctors determined that she needed a c-section, and of course she felt deflated after many hours of attempting to deliver her baby vaginally. By the time her baby was born, she had labored around 3 days total.

I cried on my way home. And I cried hard. I felt so sorry for my client, imagining how I would feel under the same circumstances. And with all of the faith I could muster, I prayed that God would heal her heart and prevent her from being traumatized from her birth experience. I prayed that God would teach her whatever lessons were in that experience for her to learn, and that she would emerge a better Christian and a better woman. I also asked that God would fill her with joy. Quite honestly, I felt like I only had faith the size of a mustard seed on this one, not big faith.

To my amazement, when I went to her home after her hospital stay, I realized that God had answered "yes"! I asked her how she felt after processing her birth story. And she told me what God taught her and that she realized her stubbornness led her to learn the hard way sometimes. Despite the hard lesson, she was grateful for her journey. And she could already identify God's purpose in the sequence of events.

This new mama was glowing! She radiated the joy of the Lord and hardly stopped smiling the entire time I was at her house. My client did not appear traumatized at all!

And when I asked for confirmation of that, she verified that she, indeed, felt gratitude and joy, but no trauma.

Circumstances were not ideal, but we serve an intentional God. When you invite Him into hard situations, His presence is powerful. God never abandoned Client #9, and she felt that in her soul. He kept her soul in peace during the same circumstances that lead some others to feel traumatized. God does not need perfection from people or from situations in order to birth beauty. With surrender, prayer, and worship, you'll be amazed at how resilient and unshakeable you can be.

Appendix E
Prayers for Childbirth

Conception

Heavenly Father, in the name of Jesus, I ask that You help me conceive a child in Your perfect timing. Touch the reproductive organs of both me and my husband with Your mighty power, making our bodies function according to Your design for conception. I pray, Lord, that You will keep my unborn child free from deformities, severe allergies, diseases, disorders, mental illness, and demonic possession.

(The following paragraph can be prayed both before **conception** and during **pregnancy**.)

Lord, please touch every gene and cell in my and my husband's body, and keep us from passing down any genes that lead to sickness or sin. Make us pass down generational blessings, and break any curses off our lives. Help us pass down only genes that lead to life, godliness, and health, in Jesus' name. Please prepare our hearts to be ready for parenthood when that time comes. Give us patience for the wait and grace for the journey! In Jesus' name, amen.

Pregnancy

Lord God, touch every cell, organ, limb, appendage, and system of my baby's body with perfect health and wholeness, in Jesus' name. I command my baby's brain to develop perfectly and function normally and be advanced with great intelligence and a high IQ, in Jesus' name. I command my baby's heart to be whole and healthy, in Jesus' name. I speak to my baby's respiratory system to function smoothly.

Heavenly Father, please protect my baby from all adverse effects of genetically modified organisms, pesticides, radiation, vaccines, and all forms of environmental toxins.

Lord, please prevent my child from developing diseases, disorders, mental illness or identity confusion of any kind. Please prevent my child from ever being a victim of physical abuse, sexual abuse, emotional abuse, or crime. Give my child a repentant heart so that he/she will be quick to change when necessary.

Keep this pregnancy in perfect health with adequate amniotic fluid levels, sufficient placental transfer of nourishment to my baby, healthy blood sugar and blood pressure levels, and with all of my organs and baby's organs functioning well. Please help my baby's development to be healthy, smooth, and timely, in Jesus' name. Make my baby grow at a healthy rate and with all body parts in normal proportion and quantity.

Lord, I pray that You will empower me to fight toxic

thoughts and emotions that are harmful to this pregnancy in physical and spiritual ways. Fill me with joy and gratitude, triggering hormonal responses in my body that aid proper development of my baby, both physically and spiritually.

Father, in the name of Jesus Christ, I dedicate this baby to You. My baby is marked for the Kingdom of God–righteousness, peace, and joy in the Holy Ghost. Please fill my entire bloodline with Your light, love, and peace, drawing each of us to intimate relationship with You daily. Help my baby to know who You've called him/her to be at an early age and show me and my baby's father what gifts/talents to nurture. Lead my baby to a purpose-driven life at a young age, shining your light and love even before elementary school.

Please fill my baby with Your Holy Spirit, like You did with John the Baptist while he was in Elizabeth's womb (See Luke 1:15, 39-45). In Jesus' name, amen.

Labor & Delivery

Lord, I ask You to breathe upon my labor and delivery experience. Please anchor my soul in You so deeply that nothing can shake me. Strengthen me spiritually and physically for the adventure. Help my labor and delivery to be smooth, peaceful, and time-efficient. Please help my labor to progress at a remarkable pace without any stalls or regressions.

Touch my cervix, uterus, pelvis, and all connected ligaments, muscles, and tissues, and make them all do their jobs perfectly according to Your design for childbirth. Please enable me to experience physiological childbirth from early labor all the way through delivery of the placenta. Keep my perineum, vagina, and labia intact with no tears. Prevent my pelvic floor muscles from experiencing trauma and help these muscles to recover quickly.

Give me wisdom to know who should be present for my labor and delivery. Help me to build my birth support team according to wisdom and knowledge. Lead me to where I should give birth and work it out so that the right medical staff is on-call at the time of my birth. Protect me and my baby from any birth professionals who would bring physical or spiritual harm or who would operate in detrimental ignorance, incompetence, or evil of any kind.

Help me to labor FEARLESSLY, in Your perfect peace. Please bless me to experience the JOY of bringing forth new life in the absence of unbearable pain, sorrow, or trauma. Flood me with Your peace and gratitude, and display Your power during my birth story. In the mighty name of Jesus, amen!

Postpartum

Lord, in the name of Jesus, I ask that You will touch my postpartum season. Help my body recover supernaturally quickly. And if there's anything in my soul that needs healing after delivery, heal my soul supernaturally quickly, too! Prevent me from experiencing any postpartum health complications. Keep me and my baby in perfect health, preventing us from all types of injuries, disorders, and diseases, even down to the common cold.

Fill me with Your joy, shielding me from experiencing the baby blues or any kind of postpartum mood or anxiety disorder. Touch my hormones, balancing them to aid in my peace and happiness. Help me to experience a beautiful birth high that lasts for several weeks!

Fill me and my baby's father with Your grace for parenthood, including all of the adventures, inconveniences, and fatigue. Fuel our souls with grace, peace, and love. May Your grace empower us to overcome the challenges with greater ease. And may Your love cover the imperfections of this season. Love through us in such a way that the difficulties pale in comparison to the joys of this postpartum season.

Help me see my body through Your eyes. And empower me to care for my body according to wisdom.

Grant my breastfeeding journey with great success even from the beginning. Keep my nipples from cracking or bleeding; help me to apply wisdom with breastfeeding techniques; and help my baby to learn quickly and latch properly. Bless my milk supply with all of the abundance my baby needs, and help me to operate in wisdom managing my milk supply. Give me the strength both physically and emotionally to remain faithful to our breastfeeding journey for as long as my baby needs.

Send supportive people to surround my growing family. Send people who will bless us with love, encouragement, acts of kindness, food, house chores, and babysitting. Build our village and help me to manage stress wisely and recover quickly and joyfully ... All in Jesus' name I pray, amen!

Appendix 9
Scriptures to
Birth Like You Believe

(My revisions are in brackets.)

Purpose

1. Psalm 127:3-5a (NLT) "Children are a gift from the LORD; they are a reward from him. Children born to a young [woman] are like arrows in a warrior's hands. How joyful is the [woman] whose quiver is full of them!"

Faith

1. Matthew 19:26b (KJV) "With men this is impossible; but with God all things are possible."
2. Matthew 17:20b (ESV) "If you have faith like a grain of mustard seed, you will say to this

mountain, 'Move from here to there,' and it will move, and nothing will be impossible for you."

Fear

1. 1 John 4:18 (NKJV) "There is no fear in love; but perfect love casts out fear, because fear involves torment. But [she] who fears has not been made perfect in love."
2. 2 Timothy 1:7 (NKJV) "For God has not given us a spirit of fear, but of power and of love and of a sound mind."

Joy

1. Psalm 16:11 (NKJV) "You will show me the path of life; In Your presence is fullness of joy; At Your right hand are pleasures forevermore."
2. Psalm 16:8-9 (ESV) "I have set the LORD always before me; because he is at my right hand, I shall not be shaken. Therefore my heart is glad, and my whole being rejoices; my flesh also dwells secure."

Prayer

1. Philippians 4:6-7 (NKJV) "Be anxious for nothing, but in everything by prayer and supplication, with thanksgiving, let your requests be made known to God. And the peace of God, which surpasses all understanding, will guard your hearts and minds through Christ Jesus."
2. John 16:24b (NKJV) "Until now you have asked nothing in My name. Ask, and you will receive, that your joy may be full."
3. Matthew 21:22 (NKJV) "And whatever things you ask in prayer, believing, you will receive."

4. James 5:16b (NKJV) "The effective, fervent prayer of a righteous [woman] avails much."

5. Matthew 7:7-11 (NKJV) "Ask, and it will be given to you; seek, and you will find; knock, and it will be opened to you. For everyone who asks receives, and [she] who seeks finds, and to [her] who knocks it will be opened. Or what man is there among you who, if his son asks for bread, will give him a stone? Or if he asks for a fish, will he give him a serpent? If you then, being evil, know how to give good gifts to your children, how much more will your Father who is in heaven give good things to those who ask Him!"

6. Mark 11:24 (NKJV) "Therefore I say to you, whatever things you ask when you pray, believe that you receive them, and you will have them."

7. 1 John 5:14-15 (NKJV) "Now this is the confidence that we have in Him, that if we ask anything according to His will, He hears us. And if we know that He hears us, whatever we ask, we know that we have the petitions that we have asked of Him."

For Exhaustion/Discouragement

1. Psalm 61:2b (NKJV) "When my heart is overwhelmed; Lead me to the rock that is higher than I."

2. 2 Corinthians 12:9a (NKJV) "My grace is sufficient for you, for My strength is made perfect in weakness."

3. Isaiah 40:29-31 (NKJV) "He gives power to the weak, And to those who have no might He increases strength. Even the youths shall faint and

be weary, And the young men shall utterly fall, But those who wait on the LORD Shall renew their strength; They shall mount up with wings like eagles, They shall run and not be weary, They shall walk and not faint."

Strength

1. Psalm 91:1-2 (NKJV) "[She] who dwells in the secret place of the Most High Shall abide under the shadow of the Almighty. I will say of the LORD, 'He is my refuge and my fortress; My God, in Him I will trust.'"

2. Psalm 18:28-32a (ESV) "For it is you who light my lamp; the LORD my God lightens my darkness. For by you I can run against a troop, and by my God I can leap over a wall. This God—his way is perfect; the word of the LORD proves true; he is a shield for all those who take refuge in him. For who is God, but the LORD? And who is a rock, except our God?—the God who equipped me with strength ..."

3. Psalm 27:1 (KJV) "The LORD is my light and my salvation; whom shall I fear? the LORD is the strength of my life; of whom shall I be afraid?"

4. Psalm 18:1-2, 46 (ESV) "I love you, O LORD, my strength. The LORD is my rock and my fortress and my deliverer, my God, my rock, in whom I take refuge, my shield, and the horn of my salvation, my stronghold. The LORD lives, and blessed be my rock, and exalted be the God of my salvation."

Trust

1. Psalm 91:4 (KJV) "He shall cover thee with his feathers, and under his wings shalt thou trust: his truth shall be thy shield and buckler."
2. Psalm 112:7 (NLT) "[The godly] do not fear bad news; they confidently trust the LORD to care for them."
3. Psalm 28:7 (ESV) "The Lord is my strength and my shield; in Him my heart trusts, and I am helped. My heart exults, and with my song I give thanks to Him."

Appendix G
Confessions for Birth

(#1) **Fearless**: I will approach my childbirth FEARLESSLY. I am a daughter of God, the Most High. He is powerful, and I am powerful in Him. He is able to do exceedingly, abundantly, above what I can ask or think. I am bold, confident, excited, and at peace in my Lord. My mind is fixed on Jesus. I can do all things through Christ who strengthens me.

(#2) **My Co-Laborer:** I am not alone. The Almighty is co-laboring with me. He stands with me as my Rock and my Fortress. He carries the load with me. He's a good God, and He lives in me. He is always here. I can do all things through Christ who strengthens me. His mighty hands are holding me now. His angels are surrounding me.

(#3) **My Authority:** Hormones and emotions, you will remain in line with the Spirit of God and His Word. The Word has preeminence in my life and authority over my body and emotions. My hormones and emotions are subject to Your Word. My body is subject to me; I am not subject to my body. I use the name of Jesus to make my body do what it needs to do.

(#4) **Made for This:** I was MADE to do this. God specially and uniquely designed my body for childbirth. I have everything I need already inside of me. My body is in line with God's plan. My body is functioning perfectly to deliver this baby and placenta the way He created me to. He made no mistakes in my body. Before I was born, He knew the size of my baby and the size of my body. God is not surprised by anything.

(#5) **Laboring for Love:** Creator God delights in bringing forth new life. It is not His will that I approach childbirth with fear or dread. That is the world's way, rooted in the curse because of sin. I will approach childbirth God's way, with the thrill and joy of bringing forth new life. What beauty and wonder–that God has created a new life inside my womb! I joyfully anticipate laboring for love.

(#6) **Power:** Because the Holy Spirit lives in me, I already have the supernatural power I need for a peaceful childbirth in the glory of God, in the holy of holies … in the secret place of the Most High, under the shadow of His wings. The curse of sorrow in childbirth is broken from my life, and I am free to experience childbirth the way God originally intended before sin entered the world. "Where the Spirit of the Lord is, there is freedom"–2 Corinthians 3:17b (ESV).

(#7) **Trust in God:** Lord, I put my trust in You; no other help I know. No one else can touch the inner workings of my body and mind like You can. I need You. Right now, I rest in You. I trust my soul, body, and baby in Your hands. My whole body is relaxed and at peace in the sovereignty of You.

(#8) **Body:** My body is 100% relaxed, open, stretchy, and obedient to God. My soul is at rest in this divine time. My cervix is smoothly [48]effacing and dilating to 10 cm, and my pelvis is opening at the best angles for my baby's descent. My vagina and perineum are stretching gracefully, without tearing, in Jesus' name. I am not afraid.

(#9) **Holy Spirit Invitation:** I invite the glory of God in this place. Holy Spirit, You are welcome here. I know that You inhabit my praises, not my complaints, moans, or groans. So, I praise You! I worship You! I adore You! Show me Your glory, Lord.

(#10) **Thanksgiving:** In this moment, I glorify Creator God. I dedicate my labor zone as a worship zone. Thank You for this atmosphere of perfect love, peace, power, and strength. Thank You for my faith. And thank You for being here with us. Your presence is irreplaceable and unmistakable.

(#11) **God's Glory:** Angels are all around me and my baby everywhere we go. The glory of God is here as I offer pure, surrendered worship. God is WITH me, and I am not afraid. God is here. In the presence of the Lord is fullness of joy. I have no sorrow. God is love, and perfect love casts out fear. I am fearless in Christ.

A message God spoke to me during my prayer time while pregnant with my first child:

"Rest in Me. I will deliver this baby, says the Lord. I am your Deliverer. I Am that I Am. The weight of this is not on you. I created this child within you, and I will deliver her from your womb out into this world and into your arms. I am the Creator and Deliverer. Trust Me for it. I will come through."

---

[48] Effacement (noun): the thinning and shortening of the cervix during labor

Appendix H
Definitions

1. Cervix (noun): the opening of the uterus, located on the bottom of the uterus. This is where babies exit the uterus during labor.
2. Dilation (noun): the opening or widening of the cervix during labor to make enough space for babies to exit the uterus
3. Doula (noun): a birth professional who supports women and their partners physically, educationally, and emotionally during pregnancy, labor, and the early postpartum period. Doulas provide comfort techniques for labor, birth plan preparation and implementation, advocacy, and holistic birth support. They are professionals who work only for the mother and are not typically employed by a hospital or birth center.
4. Effacement (noun): the thinning and shortening of the cervix during labor

5. Fear-mongering (noun): manipulation that exaggerates risks to evoke fear in the victim to persuade him/her towards a targeted decision

6. Midwife (noun): a medical professional who delivers babies of low-risk pregnancies and performs clinical tasks for childbirth, specializing in vaginal birth and natural techniques for delivery

7. Obstetrician (noun): a surgeon who specializes in medical interventions for childbirth and is trained to manage both high-risk and low-risk pregnancies from a medical perspective

8. Perinatal (adjective): the period of time spanning pregnancy and the postpartum season

9. Perineum (noun): the tissue connecting a woman's vagina and anus. This is the area that people refer to when they describe the "ring of fire" during the pushing stage. The "ring of fire" describes the burning/stinging sensation of the perineum as the baby's head stretches mom's tissues in the process of delivery.

10. Physiological (adjective): unmedicated, vaginal childbirth without medical interventions

11. Pitocin (noun): a drug that seeks to mimic the naturally-occuring effects of the oxytocin hormone on the uterus. It is synthetic oxytocin, called by other names in various countries (e.g. Syntocinon). Pitocin is used in childbirth to medically induce (start) labor, to accelerate labor contractions, and used to prevent or treat hemorrhage during or after the delivery of the placenta.

    a. (The reason some moms are afraid of receiving Pitocin is that it can make contractions feel unnaturally strong; it increases the risk of uterine rupture and hyperstimulation of the uterus; it counteracts the flow of natural oxytocin; and it increases the temptation to request medicinal pain relief.)

12. Postpartum (adjective or adverb): the period following childbirth

Acknowledgments

First, I must thank God. My Heavenly Father is the One who urged me to write *Birth Like You Believe* in the midst of a very busy season of my life. Between my roles as a wife, mother, staff pastor at Word of Faith Family Worship Cathedral, and as a labor doula and childbirth educator, only God could have led me to add another major project to my task list. And, He did!

Through a dream and prophetic words and visions from others, I knew that writing this book was a God-assignment. I didn't want to invest this much time into something that was a "good" thing but not a "God" thing. God truly clarified His will to me and gave me the confirmation I needed. He is the driving force of my soul, my anchor, and my master. Whatever He says "do," I do my best to complete!

Next, I must thank my husband. Kyle, I appreciate the practical ways you support me and the stability and safety you bring to our home. Your love uplifts me, grounds me, and balances me. Dreams like the publication of this book would be much more challenging to achieve without the roots of your love helping my soul to flourish.

Also, I want to thank my biggest cheerleader: my twin sister, Kristie. Any dream I have, you encourage. You believe in me, and that puts fuel in the tank of my soul. Before I wrote a single chapter, you affirmed me and had no doubt that the product would be exactly what God destined it to be. I don't know what I would do without you, Twin, and I don't ever want to find out, haha!

To my parents: You two are the wind beneath my wings and the giants on whose shoulders I stand. The foundation you've laid for me continues to drive me to achieve every dream God places in my heart. Without you two, there is no me. Thank you for the excellence, righteousness, and love of who you are. And thank you for building my life with the best of what God has given to you!

To my previous clients: Thank you for trusting me to support you in the most special, vital of life's milestones! The content of this book has been enhanced by what God has taught me and shown me through my experiences with each of you.

About The Author

Nicknamed "The Praying Doula," Kirstie Foley specializes in comfort for the body and soul, combining both physical techniques and spiritual support for pregnancy and labor.

Kirstie is a labor doula, childbirth educator, ordained minister, worship leader (singer), author, and preacher. She is the founder and owner of Powerful Peace Doula Care, and she is a staff pastor. She serves at Word of Faith Family Worship Cathedral in Austell, Georgia, under the leadership of her father and senior pastor, Bishop Dale C. Bronner.

Most importantly, she is a devoted servant of Jesus Christ, a loving wife to Kyle Foley, and the proud mother of two beautiful children, Elaina and Elias.

Both of her births were unmedicated, the first in a hospital and the second at home (a water birth). Thankfully, Kirstie experienced what she describes as "powerful peace" during both of her labors–quite the opposite of birth trauma. Consequently, she is passionate about helping others experience powerful peace in childbirth, no matter the outcome.

Kirstie has always been dedicated to excellence. In 2013, she and her identical twin sister, Kristie, became nationally acclaimed as the co-valedictorians of Spelman College, with matching 4.0 GPA's. And in 2014, they published their first book, *Double Vals: The Keys to Success in College and Life Beyond*. Their story has been featured in numerous media sources, including ABC World News with Diane Sawyer, Fox & Friends, Fox 5, *The Atlanta Journal Constitution*, *Essence Magazine*, *Ebony Magazine*, National Public Radio, Radio One, and Emory University's radio.

Additionally, after working as youth and young adult pastors and youth event coordinators for several years, Pastors Kirstie and Kristie published their second book, *Bridging the Gap: What Teens Wish Their Parents Knew*.

Kirstie does inspirational speaking for churches, women's conferences, schools, non-profit organizations, and other events.

Committed to Jesus, family, and Kingdom business, Pastor Kirstie Foley is always ready for where prayer and obedience will take her next!

www.powerfulpeacedoula.com
www.kirstieandkristie.com
www.woffamily.org

Other Books By

Kirstie Bronner Foley

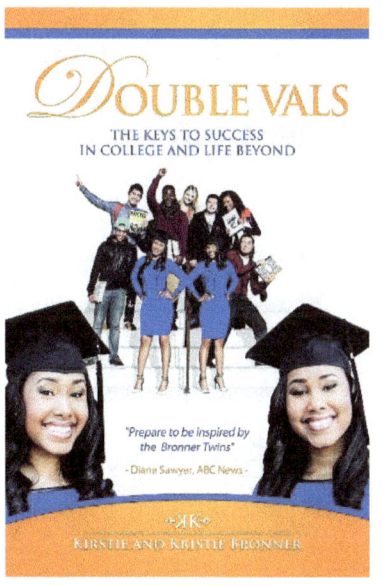

Kirstie (Bronner) Foley and Kristie (Bronner) Brawley graduated from Spelman College in 2013 as the double valedictorians with matching 4.0 GPA's. In *Double Vals*, Kirstie and Kristie share the secrets to their success in college, which they still use in life today. Join them as they colorfully illuminate their college journey infused with powerful keys that will enrich your daily habits!

You'll learn the keys to…

- Study tips that work miracles
- Time management that makes you a master of minutes
- Scheduling that conquers busyness

- Relationships that boost your GPA
- Perspective that redirects your focus
- Excellence that causes you to stand out
- Risks that you *should* take
- Balanced living that yields holistic health
- Classroom miracles that drop your jaw
- School lessons that transfer to life lessons

Purchase *Double Vals: The Keys to Success in College and Life Beyond* on www.kirstieandkristie.com.

$15.99 Paperback
ISBN: 978-0-9891356-8-9

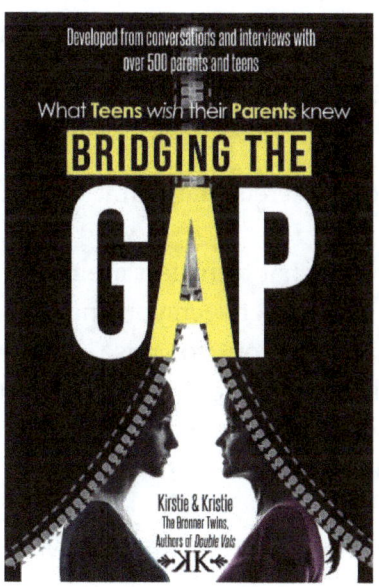

Have you ever wished you could get the inside scoop on your teenager's brain?—What they're thinking, why they make such foolish choices, and why they just don't listen? Well, this insight is the driving force behind *Bridging the Gap: What Teens Wish Their Parents Knew.*

Of all the parenting books you might have read, what makes this one special is just how Kirstie and Kristie have attained their inside scoop. Surprisingly, they have never parented teens, but they are simply twin sisters who grew up in a household of seven and spent most of their career with the interesting species we call teenagers.

They've engaged teens and their parents enough to see the patterns, the dead-end mistakes, and the things that really work. In Bridging the Gap, they share insight from interviews they've conducted with parents and teens separately; their perspective of what their parents did right; and stories from countless sessions with teens. Kirstie and Kristie don't claim to have the cure for every household, but they are confident that, if you apply these principles, you'll be better prepared to cultivate an exceptional family.

You'll discover secrets that will...

- Expose what teenagers are really thinking
- Build trust between you and your teen
- Empower you to raise powerful decision-makers instead of immature robots
- Heal your parent-teen relationship
- Help you discipline without driving your teen away
- Enhance communication between you and your teen
- Teach the balance of being "friend" and "parent"
- Increase your teen's respect for you
- Create healthy boundaries for protection
- Help you protect without smothering
- Improve your teen's self-image

"Time to change the game and bridge the gap between you and your teen!"

Purchase *Bridging the Gap: What Teens Wish Their Parents Knew* on www.kirstieandkristie.com.

$17.99 Paperback
ISBN: 978-1-7332156-0-2